WHITCHURCH STOUFFVILLE PUBLIC LIBRARY

WS546365

WITHDRAWN

D1084271

AUG 1 8 2015

BITS

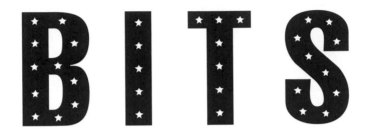

BITS

A Comedy Writer's Screams of Consciousness

Preface by Carol Burnett

KENNY SOLMS

PROSPECTA PRESS

WESTPORT AND NEW YORK

2015

WHITCHURCH-STOUFFVILLE PUBLIC LIBRARY

Copyright © 2014 by Kenneth Alan Solms

All rights reserved. No portion of this book may be reproduced in any fashion, print, facsimile, or electronic, or by any method yet to be developed, without express written permission of the publisher.

Published by
Prospecta Press
An imprint of Easton Studio Press
P.O. Box 3131
Westport, CT 06880
(203) 571-0781
www.prospectapress.com

Book and cover design by Barbara Aronica-Buck

Hardcover ISBN: 978-1-63226-016-1
E-book ISBN: 978-1-63226-017-8
First edition

Printed in the United States of America
First printing January 2015

This is dedicated to my brother, Stephen Solms,
who kept me laughing all my life.

Special thanks to Jeffrey Ashkin, Jake Schaefer, and David Wilk
for all their assistance in making *Bits* a reality.

And to my favorite people of all, comedy writers.
Let's have lunch. I'm sure we'll all meet
one day when our table is ready.

Preface

Kenny Solms and I have been joined at the hip for more than forty-seven years. You would think by now I would have grown tired of laughing, but I haven't . . . and never will. His "bits," like all his comedy inventions, are always fresh, always surprising, and never mean. Sort of like a whoopee cushion on an electric chair.

"Kenny . . . Kenny . . . Kenny . . . " That's me after one of his bits. "Thank you . . . Thank you . . . Thank you . . . " That's me after reading this wonderful memoir. He has modestly entitled it *Bits*, but we, his audience and friends, would have more appropriately entitled it *Boulders*, as in "boulders of laughter." To work with Kenny is to laugh with Kenny. That is not to say he didn't work hard (I made sure of that.) But anytime a writer shows up in the female star's clothes, you know it's not show business as usual.

If I had to drive across the country and I had Kenny in the car, I wouldn't need a radio. And I'd much rather listen to Kenny nonstop and have entertainment galore across the fruited plain. (As I write this, I can hear Kenny riffing on "fruited plain" for about a hundred miles.) But this is supposed to be a preface and not a eulogy. So, dear reader, you have in your hands the closest thing to having Kenny Solms in your car. Read on and enjoy the distinct pleasure of his company, as I have for all these many years. And believe me, I'm "so very glad we had those times together."

— Carol Burnett

Contents

BITS

THE EARLY YEARS

I've been doing bits ever since I can remember. Anything to get attention. Anything to get noticed. Anything to get laughs. Needy? You bet! And then some. I had no choice. My older brother was always the center of attention, and not in a good way. He was always getting into trouble, so he was always the focus at the dinner table. I tried to get attention but he was a lot of competition. I guess that's when I started doing bits. Anything to distract. Anything to break people up while my brother was breaking dishes. Doing bits was how I got through life. It's always been too hard for me to take the world seriously. So I've always laughed through it all whether I meant to get a laugh or not.

One of my first bits was actually unintentional. I was in second grade performing in my first school play. I kept studying the script, looking at it but not understanding the joke. I didn't see anything funny about it. I was confused right until the time I walked onto the stage. I'll never forget it. I was playing a genie. Nice, huh? Even then, you wouldn't find me in the leading man breakdowns. They always used to call my type "character actor"—even at age five. This is what happened. Here's my entrance: "Laughing and jumping. Hi everybody," I said. I didn't hear a laugh. I even had the nerve to try the line again. And louder this time. "Laughing and jumping. Hi everybody." Still no laugh. It was that horrible silence when you know you've just bombed. Now I tried a little movement. Then a lot of movement.

Big expressions, funny walk. I even considered dropping my pants. My teacher finally explained why I didn't get a laugh. It seemed "laughing and jumping" was in parentheses and wasn't meant to be spoken out loud. They were directions and I was reading them. The directions. "Laughing and jumping." "Laughing and jumping." It was humiliating. Bombing on your first entrance ever.

But months later, I had a comeback. This too was unintentional. It was at the school spelling bee which took place in the big auditorium. Each class was represented by its best speller. It wasn't a show or anything, but I loved being onstage. Too bad: I wasn't onstage for long. On my very first word, there was a problem. The word was, "advertisement." It was a no-brainer. I started slowly: "A-D-V-E-R-T-I-S-E." This would be a cinch. And then I heard a laugh. And then another. And another. Being class clown, I was used to getting laughs. But I hadn't done or said anything funny yet. Why was everybody laughing? I was just trying to spell "advertisement" correctly and move on. The laughter confused me. Maybe, I wasn't spelling the word correctly after all. So I gave it another stab. "Advertisement. A-D-V-E-R-T-I-S," I continued. Another laugh rang out. Ah, they were trying to help me. The audience was trying to warn me. Obviously, I was going to go for an "e" but the laughs indicated maybe I should perhaps drop the "e." So I ripped right through it. "A-D-V-E-R-T-I-S-M-E-N-T," I proudly spelled out. And then I heard, "Sorry, Kenny, that is incorrect." When I had paused, the kids must have thought I was doing a bit. I thought they were warning me to drop the "e." Oh my God! The first one out! I had to sit down for another forty minutes. Dwarfed by the lucky ones still in the competition, I was soon joined by that idiot Dennis Zuckerman, who screwed up on the word "chasm," stupidly spelling it, C-H-A-S-E-M. He had added an "E". Now I was happy. I had company. Another loser.

It was a tough loss. That auditorium was a big room to bomb in. I needed to bounce back but in a big way. This time the bits would be intentional. Then it dawned on me. I'll play the cafeteria. The whole school would be eating out of my hand—literally. I devised a way to sell milk there so I had a never-ending line of buyers with a joke for each. But eventually, they closed me down. Selling chocolate milk in machines killed my business. But I was determined to have a comeback.

And boy, did I! Just like Jack Nicholson, Tom Hanks, Bette Davis, I kept nailing down all the awards that were there to get. I won "Best Sense of Humor" in my yearbook. And "Peppiest." Nowadays, they call that A.D.D. As if I needed more attention, I also became the school mascot, the panther. That meant I ran around the football field a lot blocking everyone's views of the plays, but cheering like crazy. I had no inhibitions. "Boomalaka, boomalaka sis-boom-bah, Cheltenham High School, rah rah rah," I screamed. Anything to get attention. I loved it until the day my father came to the big football game to see his son, the panther. I thought I was going to die when I spotted him. What was he doing there? He couldn't have thought I was playing in the game. I immediately hid behind the panther papier-mâché mask as if he wouldn't notice me. God, when he finally saw me! What must he have been thinking? All the other boys were out there on the field catching balls, tackling. Then there's his son, the panther, cart-wheeling and prancing with all the girls. What an image. It was as if my life was a constant campaign for the Oscars. Get attention, create a buzz and then just like in an old Hollywood movie, a miracle happened.

Mike Nichols and Elaine May came to my junior high school. Yes, *the* Mike Nichols and Elaine May. The famous duo. What the hell were they doing in a suburb outside of Philadelphia? As it turned out, they were trying out material for their upcoming Broadway debut. They probably wanted to be as far away as possible from New York City and any human beings who even knew who they were. But I knew who they were, didn't I? I had seen them on a Sunday afternoon TV show called *Omnibus*. They instantly became my idols. They had changed my life. Their characters and their targets were everything I laughed at too. My high school girlfriend, Marlene Weinstock, adored them as well. She was in as much shock as I was when we sneaked into the auditorium that afternoon to watch them rehearse. We even had the nerve to introduce ourselves to them as if we were on some equal level or something. It was even worse than that. We started doing their lines *to them*. "Information does not argue with a closed mind," I bellowed out, and Marlene dramatically added, "Bartok died on Central Park West"—lines from their first album. The nerve. They looked at us as if we were crazy, and we were. They weren't *our* lines. They were *their* lines. And there we were, doing them. They couldn't get away from us fast enough.

Kenny with Nichols & May and Marlene

But it got crazier. Months later at a school show, we actually lip-synched their routines off their now celebrated comedy album. We were so unoriginal. So tacky. But when our friends said they liked us, we said thank you, as if we were *the* Mike and Elaine. Years later, I was lucky enough to meet Elaine May . . . again. As if she would remember me. I told her the high school story and once again, she walked away even faster than she did the first time.

School was a fun time for me. Not for my teachers, though. Bits, bits, bits. One time in math class, I was doing just a few too many bits and my teacher, Mr. Taddei, picked me up in his arms, deposited me in the trash can in the hallway, and made me stay there all day. The funny part is I liked it. I got more laughs in the trash than in the class. I got dirty too.

Even when I went to camp, I was still performing. Maybe it's because I was the only one in the bunk who wasn't wearing dental retainers on my teeth and could actually speak. Of course most of the retainers ended up in the lake by the end of the summer along with forty pairs of eyeglasses, seventeen contact lenses and the occasional camper. Since the camp was in Maine, all the campers took the night train from Philadelphia to Portland with stopovers in New York for our rich New York campers and one idiot who made the train stop in Stamford, Connecticut, because his parents didn't want to drive into the city that day. We all wore camp uniforms. Each department store had a camp section where pennants hung everywhere. Takajo, Brunonia, Nehoc (that's "Cohen" spelled backwards), and ours—Powhatan.

The camp put saltpeter, a curb on the libido, in all the food. I guess they didn't want us attacking each other, although it was an all-boys camp. I always wondered why a seven-year-old kid would need saltpeter. One counselor was rumored to like it. Years later it made sense. He was the arts and crafts counselor.

I went to that camp for ten years. That's about $10,000 and that didn't include candy and stamps, for which they charged a whopping a $175 extra.

The lake was beautiful. Well, it looked beautiful. I can count the times I went in it. It was freezing. I used to fake it. I would take a shower, then still wet, run onto the dock and say to the counselor, "Water's great today, good to see you." Some kids even went in for a morning dip as if they wanted to get their money's worth out of the lake. Not me.

I was show business even then. I wrote the bunk song to the tune of "There Is Nothing Like a Dame" from *South Pacific*.

WE HAVE SEVEN IN OUR BUNK.
THE FINEST THEY DO SAY.
RONNY, JEFF AND JIMMY.
BERT, JOHNNY, KENNY AND JAY.
WE HAVE THE CLEANEST BUNK.
MUCH CLEANER THAN THE REST.
WHAT ARE WE CALLED? WE'RE CALLED THE BEST.
THERE IS NOTHING LIKE BUNK FOUR.
NOTHING IN THIS CAMP.
THERE IS NOTHING LIKE BUNK FOUR.
THERE IS NOTHING LIKE BUNK FOUR.

I couldn't think of a better ending for the song but we still won the contest for best bunk song. On Parents' Night I did Carmen Miranda's "Cuanto La Gusta." My parents must have been thrilled. While all the other boys were showing off their merit badges, I was sweating up there in full make-up. I even wanted to be famous then—not necessarily a drag queen, I just loved being on stage taking in all that applause. You see, the big thing at camp was to win the "Block P Award," the big award for all-around best camper. It was like the Oscars. You would campaign for it all summer. I tried to be the nicest, the most cooperative, to really assert myself at sport—and, in the end, I won. I was ecstatic, but it killed my brother. He went to camp for fifteen years and never won it. I still have that moldy plaque on my mantel. I couldn't resist the bit of even doing the Hollywood speech then. "There are so many people I need to thank. First of all . . . God." They were dragging me away from that campfire and I was still thanking people as I clutched the pathetic plastic lanyard.

I was really in a performing mode at my bar mitzvah. It was a formal affair at the country club: huge flowers, giant ice sculptures, the whole Jewish bit and then some. All my parent's friends and family were there in tuxedos and gowns. So were all my thirteen-year-old friends. Not only was I chatting everybody up, but I was a monster on the dance floor. But it was the live orchestra that really floored me. When I saw that twelve-piece band, I was dazzled. But how was I

Kenny with Bunk Seven. I didn't even need glasses but I liked the bit.

going to grab that microphone out of the bandleader's hand? I was already determined that this crowd had to be serenaded by me whether they wanted to be or not. I just had to figure out the right maneuver to steal that mike. Well, what was the big deal? I figured my parents were paying for it anyway. On one of his breaks, I schmoozed up the conductor and gave him my song- list. I'm glad to say I was a huge hit, doing Jolson, show tunes. I was even bold enough to take requests. Talk about bits, this was heaven. Even at thirteen I knew I had a theatrical sense. I noticed at the beginning of each orchestral set that the band played the same wonderful melody. I loved the song and that they were playing it all night. I soon discovered that it was "On The Street Where You Live" from "My Fair

Kenny and his Bar Mitzvah dates.

Lady," the acclaimed production that was trying out in Philadelphia just that week. I loved the knowhow of the orchestra sensing the song was going to be a perennial.

In high school, the bits continued. And the angles. And the short-cuts. Anything to get out of class. I was even a school monitor. You know, the student idiot who stands in the hallway and drones on and on with, "Keep going, keep going, keep going, left, right, left." That was the most boring job. That's why I jumped at the chance to work in the big time—the school store. It gave me a good stage. It gave me a good twenty minutes for bits. I also slipped my friends paper clips, candy, lunch boxes—anything to make them stay. I still have one of those lunch boxes. Should I put it on eBay? Should I put it on eBay? Who really puts any of their stuff on there? White trash selling their crap. And what is more disgusting than those garage and lawn sales? People, throw that stuff out. Why subject everyone else to those hand-me-downs? Dirty pots, pans, spatulas, old Tony Bennett albums, *Connie Francis Sings Broadway* . . .

I also worked at the school switchboard. I was right in there. Answering phones, filing report cards, changing my own. I'm kidding. No, I'm not.

Of course my acting career began in high school. I really hammed it up when I got to play Mr. DePinna in the school play, *You Can't Take It with You.* He was supposed to be a little paunchy. Needless to say I inserted a pillow under my shirt. During the play, it kept dropping, getting me laughs galore. What a scandal. The other actors must have hated me, but I loved those laughs.

The last memory of high school was the school prom. That's where you always tried to get "B.T." off your date. You remember "B.T.?" "Bare Tit." Or at least "O.T.B." Not Off Track Betting: "*Over The Bra!*" Actually, I didn't even have a date. You always ended up going to the prom with your friends. Not a girlfriend necessarily, but a friend who's a girl. Marlene, my one and only date, hit Atlantic City after the dance and I sideswiped six cars. The whole evening was a trauma. It wasn't a total loss, though. That prom night was the best sex I ever had. Too bad it wasn't with my date. I'll never tell who. Besides, it's all in my autobiographical play, *It Must Be Him*, which incidentally is available on Kindle and iPad, and if you'd like to see the play on its feet, it's also available for licensing. Just visit www.itmustbehim.com and make your selection.

KENNY GOES TO COLLEGE

I put my boomalaka high school days behind me when I attended New York University. New York City was now my campus, especially Broadway musicals and sneaking in at intermission. It's commonly called "second acting." That took a great technique. First, you'd find out exactly what time the first act broke. Then you'd mingle with the crowd on the street, grab a program, zoom in and look for any empty seats. I was even there the night Johnny Desmond replaced Sydney Chaplin in *Funny Girl*. A hysterical bit happened that night. There she was, Barbra Streisand, belting out "People" magnificently. The audience was fixated on her and apparently so was her costar, Johnny Desmond. In fact, when she finished "People," he got out of character immediately, forgetting where he was, and started applauding loudly to her. Barbra didn't know what to do. Finally, she bowed to him.

I'd even sneak friends into shows. Bring dates, make it an event. They hardly noticed that they'd miss the first act. I should mention they were also dumb. But I'd fill them in on Act One on the street. Songs, story, staging, everything . . . But that wasn't enough. I soon mastered getting into the *entire* show for free. Of course that was harder. The first way I did it was walking through the stage door, running down the stairs pretending I was a dancer. "Oh I'm so tired tonight. I hope I can dance," I complained, making sure the stage doorman heard me. The other way of getting in was really gutsy. It was called "slithering"—literally, slithering in with the crowd past the ticket taker trying not to be noticed without a ticket. Just waiting for that moment when the ticket taker started looking the other way, I'd zoom right in. See, you couldn't do this with a hit. You know, any of the sold-out shows. There was nowhere to sit once you slithered in.

Most of the nights, I saw flops. The musical version of *Exodus*, cleverly called *Ari*. The musical version of *Look Homeward, Angel*. That was called *Angel*. *Shogun*, the musical version of . . . Well, you get the idea. In a way, it gave me an education as a writer about what not to write. No musical of "Picnic." No musical of "Roman Holiday." Nowadays they musicalize every movie. Especially the folks at Disney.

Of course, I had to stop all that sneaking in once I was in the business myself. I was too frightened of getting caught. But recently, just to show off to some friends from England—you know, bragging on how easy it was—I did it again. They were going to see *Spring Awakening*, and I told them I'd join them. "Kenny, you don't have a ticket," they said. "You'll see," I told them. I was up to my old tricks. I slithered right past the ticket taker. There! I was in the theatre in an instant. Of course, two minutes later, there was a hand on my shoulder, asking me for my ticket. I said I was with the show. That didn't work. Why would it? Then I pointed to my English friends in the audience and said I was with them. I didn't know what I was saying. I was humiliated. The next thing I knew I was outside on West 45th Street, having finally lost my touch. You can't even second-act anymore. Nowadays, they ask to see your stubs if you go outside. I'll get in there again, though. You'll see. Someday, I might get arrested, but it's better than paying a $175 a ticket just to see a flop.

At NYU I majored in drama. My father hated that. He didn't want me to go into show business. Years later, I found out why. It was a big family secret, the kind that always seem to happen with Jewish families. Nobody in the immediate family knew that my father had been adopted. His real father was an actor, of all things. He wasn't a big success so maybe that's why my father was nervous. Ironically, my real grandfather had a bit part in Anita Loos's *Gentlemen Prefer Blondes*, a play I would eventually rewrite as a musical. By then my father was less worried.

Majoring in drama was a breeze. You made deals with your friends. "I'll cast you as the lead in my show if you cast me as the lead in yours," I begged. I wheeled and dealed. All very political. Before I knew it, I was the star of the drama department, literally signing autographs in the elevator and doing star bits just to get laughs. "Mr. Solms would love to see you but he's just not up to it right now," I'd moan wearily. Phony tantrum bits. "I won't go on! I won't!" I screamed.

Oh—there was another incident with my father. He and my mother drove up from Philadelphia to see their son in the big Molière play, *Tartuffe*. I'll never forget the look on his face. There I was again, Joe College, but this time in lavender tights and a tutu. And a lot of makeup. That part probably didn't surprise him.

Between my junior and senior years, I was an apprentice in summer stock near Kalamazoo, Michigan. You didn't get paid, but you got experience. For building sets and cleaning up the filthy place, they'd put you in shows. Not the huge parts. They were covered by the Actors Equity Union and paid scale to topline their shows. We were the fill-ins.

Right away, I could see that building sets was not for me. So they stuck me in the box office, where I answered the phone and sold tickets. It was a bore, but at least I didn't get paint all over me and smell of turpentine. It was well worth it to finally play a coolie with no lines in *The World of Suzie Wong*. That was a great role for me, definitely worth all the money my parents were spending on those classes at NYU. A coolie holding a rickshaw. This skinny human being could hardly carry Miss Wong, let alone the rickshaw as well. My side of the heavy rickshaw kept hitting the stage. Miss Wong hated me, as she should have. On her first big entrance, her life was in jeopardy, as the coolie carrying her could hardly pick her off the ground.

As the summer went on, I got bigger parts. The highlight for me was playing A-Rab in *West Side Story*. At maybe a hundred pounds, what a thug I made! Very threatening! My parents and brother showed up for this one too. And what an entrance they made. They had a big fight at the Philadelphia airport and arrived in separate planes. They made me so nervous that I broke out in hives and my eyes literally closed up from the swelling. But I was a trouper, and that night the show went on. Whether I could see or not was another question.

However, I knew my parents were watching. I heard them moaning. It got worse, since I could barely see, I fell into the audience. Literally. I fell into someone's lap, and they were kind enough to push

Kenny with an unhappy Suzie Wong

me back on stage. My parents were not too thrilled with that performance. They didn't even say goodbye. They didn't even stay overnight. The three of them fought all the way back to Philadelphia. What a nightmare!

The next summer was much better. I was part of an actors' repertory group somewhere in the middle of Ohio. These were shows where stars would drop in for a week's performance, and we were added to the company. I worked with Roger Smith, Pat O'Brien, Joey Brown, and William Bendix. We'd be rehearsing one new show during the day and performing another at night. My biggest role was playing a neurotic cadet, opposite Sal Mineo. He was a great guy and very funny. Of course, I always consider someone funny if they laugh at my bits, and I had Sal laughing all the time. I stayed friendly with him over the years.

But a few years later, my luck getting better parts changed. I was cast as Hugo in a touring production of *Bye Bye Birdie* starring Van

Kenny with Sal Mineo

Johnson. The tour played primarily the East Coast, so night after night there was always someone from Philadelphia in the audience. It was a little embarrassing. Too many laughs, too much applause. Too many bits. But I ate it up. Even though he never met them, Van Johnson hated my family, dreading every bravo and standing ovation I got for essentially just hamming it up. God, did I overact. The character I played was this kind of misfit who was directed to pull his sweater all the time. *Pulled* maybe, but not remotely what I did with that sweater. I pulled it down, I pulled it up, I pulled it around, in, out. It became like a story point in the show. Once again, the other actors hated me. That sweater and I kept upstaging them all night long. The director thought I was funny and never gave me a note, even though I got bigger applause than Van Johnson. A critic would say, "The most distorted performance of the century." But I liked it.

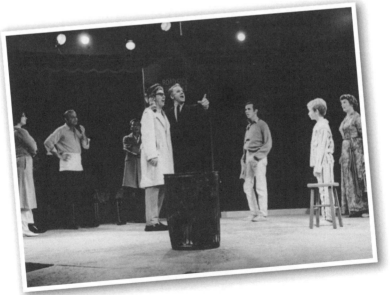

Kenny with Van Johnson

A DOLLAR A JOKE, TEN DOLLARS A SKETCH

After graduating from college, all I wanted to be was a star. I wasn't thinking about what I would do for a living. I just assumed I'd be an overnight sensation. That was a joke. I tried the Broadway audition route. One of my favorite audition songs was from *Do-Re-Mi*. Even though it was a comic song, I played it totally straight.

> OUCH! YOU'RE STEPPIN' ON MY POUCH
> TO THE BEAR SAID THE KANGAROO
> OH! YOU'RE STEPPIN' ON MY TOE
> SAID THE KANGAROO TO THE GNU.
> OUCH! MY POUCH! OH! MY TOE!
> UNK! EEK! OW! OH! OOH!
> THAT'S WHAT IS NEW AT THE ZOO!

I thought if I just did something different, I'd get noticed, and I did. But unfortunately not favorably. After a few months of rejection, I thought: there's gotta be another way. I supported myself with a part-time job at Hammacher Schlemmer, the famous specialty shop. My specialty was getting fired after three weeks.

Whenever my friends would come in, not only did I do bits but I would give them each a present. I'd just throw something in their bag. Anything off the rack. My friends loved it, but these kinds of bits didn't go over well with the folks at Hammacher Schlemmer. They told me never to grace their establishment ever again.

Still bitten by the acting bug, I soon started taking an acting class. A very prestigious one. Wynn Handman was the teacher. I even had to audition to get into it. The students were all on Broadway, so I was very impressed. When I got on stage I did my same old thing: bits. Wynn laughed and so did all the students. I don't know why they were laughing. I was just trying to act.

One of the students suggested I write comedy and said she knew a lot of comedians. She hinted that it could lead to writing jobs and even jokes for comedians. I couldn't believe it. I could actually make a living in show business by writing comedy. This is what I loved anyway—making people laugh, doing the bits. I was told comics paid a dollar a joke. My God, I thought, if I could write a thousand jokes a month, I could easily pay the rent. Ten thousand jokes a month, I could buy a townhouse. A hundred thousand, I could quit the business. The pain. The anguish. It's obvious all this thinking had already done me in. My days were numbered. The glass was half empty. Calm down. I'm doing a bit.

Writing seemed like an odd occupation. It's one thing saying funny things, but writing them down seemed bizarre. It also sounded lonely. I soon realized I needed someone to write with. I went to college with a girl named Gail Parent. We even lived in the same dorm. She was very funny. We'd always do bits at school and at parties. Even in college, we were improvising all the time and performing for our friends. It was just for fun then. Our goals were different. She wanted to get married, and I wanted to get famous. I didn't know until years later that I was the one she wanted to marry. She didn't wait, and I'm still looking. But for the answers to these and other searing questions, once again visit www.itmustbehim.com and buy the play. You'll love it. A lot of gravitas.

Finally, I asked Gail what she thought of the idea. While she found marriage and motherhood fulfilling, she already knew that she wanted more in her life. We lived miles from each other in New York, but we decided to take a stab at it. I could say we were soon killing each other, but luckily it was with laughter.

KENNY AND GAIL

A partnership can mean a lot of things. In the world of comedy, it's almost a must. It was for us. The reason is obvious. With someone in the same room, there's constant interaction. You talk all day. You laugh. You eat. You argue and it never ends. At night, you're on the phone. You run around in the same circles. You see each other at parties. We had already spent four years together in college, so we had a lot of experience. Now it was just a matter of getting it down on those yellow pads. Filling up those blank pages.

We grew up in the tail end of the Golden Age of Television, watching those great classic comedy shows: Jackie Gleason, Steve Allen, Garry Moore, *The Colgate Comedy Hour*. Gail's favorite was *The Dick Van Dyke Show*. My favorite, though, was *Your Show of Shows*, starring Sid Caesar. I used to die on Saturday night watching him in those brilliant sketches. One in particular, I never forgot. Sid was playing a tough guy in a gangster night club. Imogene Coca was the cigarette girl. All she did the entire sketch was roam around the smoky room screaming out, "Cigars, cigarettes, bullets . . . Cigars, cigarettes, bullets . . . " I roared. Gail and I already instinctively knew that things were funny in threes, that "k" is a funny letter, that you can never be too broad, and that sketch blackouts are impossible. Then there were the taboos. On television, you could never show a bathroom, especially the toilet. You could never say "pregnant." You could never show a double bed; a married couple slept on two singles. Of course, as time went on, the censors became more lenient. That was the '60s, and things were pretty tame.

The prospect of being a part of this world I was watching on television didn't escape me. If I could have squeezed into that television, I would have. While it may have been the world of laughs and make-believe, we also knew it was a real business. They were actors doing these bits. There were writers writing them. Sets were designed, music was composed. It was hard to calm down when a show was over. I remember watching Barbra Streisand on that perennial game show, *What's My Line?* and her saying how dumbfounded she was to be on the show, as it was the last program to watch on Sunday night before going to bed. I was the exact same age, and it really resonated with me, as I would take that same trip up the stairs, not looking forward to another Monday morning school-day ritual.

Our first potential buyers were the comedy team of Marty Allen and Steve Rossi. Marty was the short, tubby one whose trademark was, "Hello dere" and Steve was the handsome singer. They were the Dean Martin and Jerry Lewis of the '60s. They were constantly appearing on *The Ed Sullivan Show*, the Sunday night hit all the comedians aspired to be on. We even met Allen and Rossi "dere" backstage. It was so exciting hanging out. Stars everywhere you looked: Sammy Davis Jr., the Beatles, the Berosini Orangutans. To this day I don't know if Allen and Rossi ever really liked our material. I don't have good vibes about it. Well, who would? The orangutans had probably eaten it.

Then there was this Canadian comic Jackie Kahane, whom we wrote jokes for. That was a disaster. He sat down in front of us and read the entire monologue out loud, mostly in a dull monotone. The only other sounds were mostly his moaning, shaking his head no, and grumbling under his breath about how horrible our jokes were. So far, I figured we were behind twenty dollars in gross revenue with all the taxis and transportation just to meet these horrendous people. Joke after joke, premise after premise, comedian after comedian.

Our luck changed when we met Joan Rivers. She had just made it on *The Tonight Show Starring Johnny Carson*. Luckily, we hit it off with her famously. It was an immediate mutual attraction. We knew she was funny. She knew we were funny. We'd sit in her apartment for hours and hours. Even the way she answered the phone was hysterical. The phone would ring, she'd pick it up and say, "That's a funny line, hello, can't talk right now," and hang up. She wanted everybody who called to know she was busy. We helped her with one-liners, and she helped us with lines for sketch material. By now, Gail and I realized we wanted to do sketches rather than jokes for comedians. Maybe it was because we got paid for the sketches and people laughed at them, versus comedians who never laughed at them and we got paid nothing. A tough choice but we decided to go where the hip material was—Manhattan's esteemed Upstairs at the Downstairs.

That was the hip place for topical revues. A lot of funny people were starting to make it there at the same time. Luckily, we sold some sketches to the Upstairs. We were playing "Downstairs" doing sketches while Joan was playing "Upstairs" doing her act. She was getting very hot from her Carson buzz. Sold-out shows. Roaring audiences. I remember saying to her once, "I could get laughs too. I'm always doing bits." She glared at me and said, "Oh yeah?" Well, one night when I was up there watching her show, out of the blue she says to the audience, "Ladies and gentlemen, a wonderful friend of mine is in the audience tonight and wants to be a comedian. He even has a little routine. So let's call him up on stage." Well, I was in shock. She swore that this is what happened when I walked on stage. All you heard was, "Blah, blah, blah. Blah, blah, blah, blah, blah, blah." I don't remember it that way. In fact I think she was exaggerating. I knew I wasn't getting a lot of laughs. Basically none. But I couldn't have bombed. I couldn't have. Unless . . . Did I . . . ? Nevertheless, I learned a lesson from Joan that night. You could never tell Joan Rivers what she did was easy.

While our show was playing "Downstairs," we'd get ten dollars a week for a sketch, but we had to pay for drinks. So by the end of the month, we owed them. We were still happy to be there—not a lot of money but a lot of prestige. Upcoming talents like Madeline Kahn, Linda Lavin, and Lily Tomlin were actually saying our lines and getting laughs. My parents drove up from Philadelphia for this one too. They were going to a fancy wedding for a kid I went to high school with: Ronnie Perelman. Now he's Ronald O. Perelman, head of Revlon. My parents and their fancy friends came over for the wedding and would come to my show afterwards. Unfortunately, there was a glitch in the show that night. The cast thought it would be funny to come out at the curtain call and throw pies at each other. Well that night, they missed each other and hit—you guessed it— my parents and their fancy friends, dousing them with whipped cream. Oh, that was a scene: my father's lawyer threatening the club's manager, my mother's friend Alma Cohen pouring ice water down Lily Tomlin's dress, and me carrying my mother's now damaged suede dress around New York for a year, trying to get it covered by the club's insurance. She insisted on that, but we never collected. Too bad, the lawyers didn't

Although we still weren't making any money, we now had a prestigious manager, Bernie Brillstein, and we were represented by the equally acclaimed William Morris Agency. Bottom line: both were nightmares even though it was nice being represented.. The latter had a lot of perks—namely, free office supplies and free long-distance calls. They used to call that the "tie line." If you knew the code

Kenny with Lily

(which we immediately found out) you could call over the world, but it had to be from William Morris. Since we didn't know anybody in the world, I just called Philadelphia. "When are you coming home and getting a real job?" asked my father. "Did they pay for my dress yet?" pleaded my mother. William Morris was also famous for the "pouch." That was the huge package that flew nightly to LA and back, the '60s version of FedEx. Years later when we were working in LA and traveling to New York, we literally sent our dirty laundry back and forth in the pouch.

Brillstein got us our first odd job. Odd, to say the least. It was a gig on *The Clay Cole Hour*, a local TV disco show where high school kids danced to the hit records of the day. Gail and I had to sit off-camera and feed funny lines to the host, the amiable Clay Cole. It was a bit nerve-wracking. Let's face it, what funny thing could happen between records? We had another job on that show. When kids were sparse on the dance floor, we had to fill the empty space. Humiliating? Not as humiliating as the time we had to ask Richard Pryor what his comedy routine was going to be. I'll never forget his reaction. There was none. And he stormed out of the building. Gail and I were back on the dance floor and there was no comedian on the show that night.

However, the show paid our rent and gave us time to explore other avenues. Thank God, one came along. We sold a sketch for an upcoming Broadway revue, *Leonard Sillman's New Faces of 1968*. This was a legendary staple on Broadway and made stars of Maggie Smith, Paul Lynde, Eartha Kitt, and many more. Our out-of-town tryout was in Philadelphia, an entire two years before its debut on Broadway. Still in our early twenties, Gail and I were elated. Out of town with a Broadway show! What could be better? The answer came abruptly. Anything.

The critics panned it. I'll never forget reading those scathing

Kenny and Gail at the Clay Cole table

reviews at Philadelphia's 30th Street Station, arguing with Gail that an "impending disaster" as the review quoted, didn't mean that one really happened, did it? Sadly, it did. Two years later, the show stumbled onto Broadway and *New Faces of 1968* shuttered, as they say, after fifty-two performances. I knew enough not to invite my parents to that one. They kindly sent me the bad reviews anyway. Ironically, in William Goldman's *The Season* he praised our Miss America sketch that starred Nancie Phillips. And we didn't pay him to do that— although we certainly would have. As they say, "desperate people do desperate things."

We were very ambitious and would have done anything to keep the track of our career going upward. I wouldn't say we were starving and needing a break, as we seemed to stay constantly busy. We wrote the "Upstairs" next show of the season, wrote routines for a few new comedians along the way, and were dreaming of writing Broadway shows. A producer called us with an idea he claimed only *we* could write! The show was called, *Shubert Alley*, based on that little thoroughfare between 44th and 45 Streets that theatre-goers rushed through every night. We decided to meet with the producer. Guess where? Shubert Alley. So there we were—Gail, myself, and the producer—and guess what we did? We walked the ten seconds it takes to walk through the thoroughfare and walked back. We then went to the famed Sardi's, the theatre café right across the street. Gail and I started kicking each other under the table, as it soon became apparent that this "producer" didn't have an inkling of an idea. Nothing. Even when I brought up the name, Shubert, he confessed he had no rights to even do a story about the Shubert Brothers, the real estate tycoons who owned half of Broadway's theaters as well as Shubert Alley. So now what? I do remember quipping, "Well, there's a spot for the opening night party though—right?" He didn't even get the joke and answered flatly, "If we can get the rights."

He tried to invigorate us once more. He suggested we hang

around for a couple of hours and see what Shubert Alley was like at night, crowded, and then, hours later, empty. If he had only suggested Rockefeller Center, who knows? Or UN Plaza? Just think, if we had walked two blocks south, we could have been the team who created *42nd Street.*

OUR WEDDING ALBUM

A bout a year later, in the summer of 1966, Gail and I decided to write a comedy album on the first family, the Johnsons. We needed something big to break through nationally, something to get attention and make a mark. We certainly weren't making a fortune writing for comedians, and having our sketches performed at Upstairs at the Downstairs didn't bring in much cash.

The younger Johnson daughter was engaged to be married, and LBJ, Lady Bird, and their brood were in the newspapers and on television every day—and just ripe for satire. A few years earlier, Vaughn Meader had a huge recording success doing a comedy album on the Kennedys called *The First Family*, so maybe we should try that. When you're young and starting out, you think you can do anything. "I could sing as good as Barbra Streisand. I could even write that song 'People.' It's just one word. C'mon!" It was time to take a risk.

This was a no-brainer. The Johnsons' accents and laughable antics were bigger than life, which made them the perfect foil for satire. We pitched it to our manager, Bernie Brillstein, who thought it was a hilarious idea. "This is killer stuff. Love it. Love it. LOVE IT!" That's manager talk for, "Maybe I'll make a phone call or two." We never thought he really would, but he did indeed. He set up a meeting at Columbia Records. I guess that's how you get to Columbia Records. They never answered when I called.

Walking into CBS and meeting Goddard Lieberson, the president of Columbia Records, was an awesome experience. Even looking at the furniture was an awesome experience. I never knew there were that many colors of suede.

"Gail, did you ever see this many colors of suede in your life?"

"I never saw any suede in my life," she deadpanned.

Needless to say, we were nervous wrecks, but Bernie said, "Just go for it. Do what you always do in front of me. Just perform it. Be funny!" Easy for him to say. They always think it's so easy, as if you can just turn it on. The command makes it even worse. It's all about the moment, the timing. You can't just turn it on, but here we had no choice.

I remember it was so quiet. Lieberson was the most eminent recording producer at the time, having produced almost all the original Broadway cast musical albums, a legend in his own time—and very well dressed, I might add. I'm glad I followed my father's advice about keeping my nails properly cut. Lieberson's were immaculate and even polished, the first time I ever saw that on a man's fingers.

Bernie saw me staring at them and gave me a cue to get off the nails and just focus. I was still too nervous. I think I even added, pathetically, "Mr. Lieberson, my parents bought me the album *My Fair Lady* and I liked it very much. In fact at my bar mitzvah I first heard, 'On the Street Where You Live' and—" Bernie glared at me. I knew it was time to start pitching. Gail and I went for it.

"What should we start with?" Gail whispered.

"The Lady Bird bit."

"But the proposal scene is much funnier."

"Why? Because you wrote most of that one?"

Bernie gave us a "get on with it" stare and proceed we did.

"He's not laughing," Gail muttered.

"We just started."

"He's not even smiling."

"Gail, calm down. Just keep going."

"He's laughing now."

"That's Bernie," I snapped.

Actually, Gail was right. Lieberson was laughing as well. That's when Bernie wrapped up the meeting. "Kids, that's enough. Killer stuff. He gets the idea." And indeed he did. He even booked a studio for us and gave us a week to write and record the album, since the wedding itself was only seven days away. He wanted it to be fresh. Bernie just wanted us out of there before Lieberson could change his mind.

While we were tripping up Fifth Avenue with shock and joy, my bell-bottom pants were even ringing. Then the harsh reality set in. We only had a week. How were we ever going to do this? While invitations were being sent out for an audience, we worked our asses off. Gail even had a one-month-old infant to raise and I wouldn't let her go home. Her husband had to take up that load. Heretofore, I never understood how we could work in Gail's apartment anyway. She had just given birth. I, of course, had no clue what that meant. In fact, every time she went into her room to check on the baby, I told her, "You're spoiling Kevin." We barricaded ourselves in a friend's apartment and worked twenty-four hours a day. "No we can't go out for a bite, Gail. We can't eat. We gotta finish this sketch. Then maybe, if we have time, we'll celebrate with a half sandwich and a cup of soup."

Not only did we have to write fast, but we had to cast it at the same time. We immediately thought of comedienne Fannie Flagg for Lady Bird. Luckily, we had worked with her at Upstairs at the Downstairs, and her huge southern accent made her perfect and hilarious. When you're in a pinch for time like this, you go with friends. Luckily, we had funny ones. Not only funny but soon to be semi-household names. We cast Robert Klein as LBJ, Joanne Worley as Lynda Bird, and Gail and I played the newlyweds, Luci Baines and Pat Nugent. We weren't household names either, but we were the bosses. "Gail, let's hire ourselves," I suggested. She agreed, and we proceeded.

We soon realized this was a daunting task. We had written sketches, jokes, but never a whole album. That would be like twelve sketches. There was no question we had to do it. We were so busy writing that we didn't really think this could be a hit or even a stepping-stone. There was just too much to do, but we plowed ahead and by that Sunday we were finished except for the final cut on the wedding itself, which was happening that very day. Needless to say, we were watching every hysterical detail of it on TV, scribbling down new jokes in the script as we went along.

LYNDA BIRD: Luci, how do you feel?
LUCI BAINES: How do I look?

LYNDA BIRD: Luci, do you know about the birds and the bees?
LUCI BAINES: We're the Birds. Who are the Bees?

After we furiously wrote the last cut, we met the cast at the studio, and, before we knew it, the audience of our friends and family were in their seats. We were controlling everything and everybody. "You sit here. You sit there. Laugh. Keep laughing." We didn't even have time for a rehearsal. Once we started recording, it was clear that it was going well. Lots of laughs. Lots of applause. All very encouraging. "Gail, they're laughing," I whispered. "Those are your cousins," she muttered.

Every time Lady Bird spoke, she went into the beautification of America, no matter what the subject was. It was a running gag. Every time Fanny spoke in that hilarious Southern drawl, the audience screamed. Then we edited the album that night, and, through some miraculous occurrence, which I'll never quite understand, it was on the radio the next day. We were in shock. We'd get in taxicabs, and it was playing.

"Gail, can you believe it? They're playing the album!" I'd scream.

"Can we get royalties for that?" she asked.

What did we know? We were naïve. We asked the driver to make it louder. He wouldn't touch the dial. Why would he? After all, we were still in New York. Nobody gets impressed there. However, the album was obviously making a huge impression. It was in record stores. It was in the windows at bookstores. And if it wasn't, we slipped it in ourselves. "Just shove it in there, Gail. We don't have any money for advertising." We knew the success of the album, due to its topicality, wouldn't last long. So we had to keep moving. We were our own publicity machine.

Suddenly, Gail and I were doing appearances on local TV shows. Apparently, *Our Wedding Album*, subtitled *The Great Society Affair*, was an overnight hit. Could it be? We were in our early twenties, having just graduated college.

"Where are the tough times? Where are the hard knocks? Where's the struggle?" Gail asked, as we'd obliviously zoom off in a limousine.

Suddenly, Bernie was setting us up with agents, business managers, and publicists. It was a lot to take in but we "flowed and glowed" with the sudden success.

"Do you feel any different?" Gail constantly asked me.

"Oh I don't know," I feigned. Always going with the bit, I sighed, "Let my people get back to your people on that." The album stayed on the Billboard charts for weeks, and it definitely got the country's attention. I wish I could say the same for my parents'.

What is that all about? Why do we always want our parents' approval? Obviously, they're our first love objects. So it makes sense. But it rarely happens. Are we just shy with each other? We didn't hug and kiss a lot in my family. Withholding? Physicality was rare with us anyway. This time was no different. Was it jealousy? Was it competition? Whatever, there was no big change between us.

I'll never forget playing the album for my parents, who demanded a free copy. Can you imagine? The rest of America was buying it like it was going out of style, but not my parents. They wanted a free copy and demanded an airing. We were seated in the living room: parents, aunts, uncles in Philadelphia. The moment I put on the record, my mother shot up, asking, "Does anyone want ice cream or a soft drink?" she interrupted. I glared at her. Most of the family wasn't really listening to the album. Even though they heard the laughs, they just smiled, not laughing along. They had a look on the faces as if asking each other, "Is this funny?" I turned the album off immediately. That wasn't too soon for them. Gail's parents were worse. While they liked the album, they wondered, "What part can you dance to?"

I got more attention on *The Dating Game*. That was some experience. I was wearing a Nehru suit and sporting a moustache, answering ridiculous questions from a cocktail waitress.

GIRL: Would you like to be the first man on the moon?

KENNY: The United States of America means more to me than some fancy trip somewhere.

She thought I was serious, and I won. I was amazed. Not as amazed when I found out what the prize was. (Drum roll.) A trip to Reno and the air races. My date actually liked the sight of planes almost crashing into each other. I liked the sight of ground. It wasn't a great date. Ironically, our male escort asked me back to his room.

THE CALL

A nd then came "the call." There's always "the call," at least in movies—but in real life? Apparently. Bernie had heard from Carol Burnett and Joe Hamilton who had heard the album in sunny California. "It was selling there too?" we asked. Indeed it was. That was where Carol and her producer/husband, Joe Hamilton caught it and signed us up for their new upcoming variety show in 1967. Speaking of shock! This was getting ridiculous.

I called Gail immediately. "Carol Burnett heard our album and wants us to do her new show," I screamed into the phone. Of course, Gail flipped. Then she said, "I'm not sure I'm available. Call me back." Carol had been an idol to us. We never missed her weekly appearance on *The Garry Moore Show*. "She knew us?" I constantly asked. You never believe those kinds of things. They happen to other people, not you.

I'll never forget meeting them. They were interviewing other writers in New York and we met them at the Hilton. Gail and I were nervous wrecks. We didn't want to be late, but getting there an hour early was ridiculous. We roamed the lobby, we kept going to the bathroom, and we kept buying sundries from the gift shop. I still have the Chapstick. Finally, we went upstairs and knocked on the door. The door opened and. much to our astonishment, there was Carol, Allah-like, on her knees blessing us. "I love you two. You two are brilliant," she gushed. We didn't know what to do. We didn't know what to say.

"How do we get this woman off the floor?" I whispered to Gail. It was insane. She's the royalty here. We were the nobodies. Of course, she was adorable and warm, crawling all the way back into the living room. Joe was very funny and was wearing red socks, a tradition he continued daily. He asked us, "Do you think you can live and work in California?" I tried to be witty and, stupidly, said something like, "I don't think I can take the weather." He looked at me strangely as if he wasn't so sure he should be hiring me in first place.

Finally off the floor, Carol asked us if we were married. Gail said she was, and I cockily said, "I'm just married to our work." Carol just stared. I soon realized if I kept talking like this we could lose this job before we even started. So I spent the rest of the hour just smiling and making small talk. Very small. "What made you stay at the Hilton and not the Plaza?" They just looked at me while Gail kicked me under the table.

What can I say? I was just so nervous. It's sort of like an out-of-body experience. You're never calm. You're never really yourself. This was really Carol Burnett, a woman I adored from her genius work on *The Garry Moore Show*. Every Tuesday night, her antics were unbelievable. Everyone talked about them on Wednesday mornings. She was America's new treasure, and she was begging us to come to LA? How do you prepare for this? This was the first big star I had ever met. I didn't think success would happen this soon. While we got a taste of it with the record, this was overwhelming. Carol was so approachable and seemed like a friend from high school. She even asked me if I wanted to go with her that night to a dress rehearsal of the Tonys, where she was presenting an award. I told her I had plans. I was going to order pizza for one in my studio apartment. She laughed and invited me again. Was this really happening? Would I like to go to a rehearsal for the Tonys? Oh my God! I was in my seat before Carol was. We were watching Barbara Harris rehearse a number from a new musical, *The Apple Tree*.

I was in awe, but I was also struck by how big a fan Carol was of the proceedings. She was not remotely blasé, oohing and aahing along with me about Barbara Harris's talent. To top the day off, she took me to Sardi's afterwards, the famous theatrical restaurant haunt. It was all too magical. Was it going to continue this way? Could it be this easy? And she paid the bill too! This was the woman of my dreams.

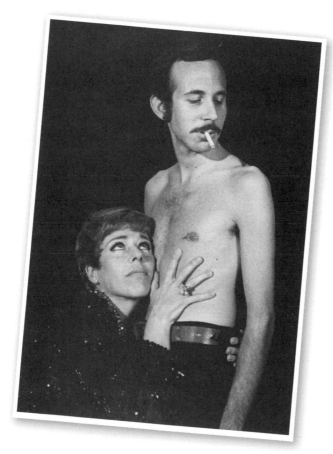

Kenny with Carol. I was obviously the man of her dreams.

STEVE ALLEN
COMEDY HOUR

L iving and studying in New York, we were always obsessed with
Broadway. So were all our friends and the people we looked
up to. That's what we always dreamed of. That's what we
always aspired to do. The bright lights, the glamour, the constant
emerging new talents, and the twenty to twenty-five new shows a season. Even writing at Upstairs at the Downstairs was a hipper thing to
be doing than weekly television: cutting satire, topicality. You
wouldn't find too much of these things on television. There was no
question that we were excited to do the Burnett show because of
Carol.

The show wasn't starting until September, so Bernie booked us
for one of those summer shows they used to have, *The Steve Allen
Comedy Hour*. This meant that Gail and I would be going out to LA
two months before we thought we were. Bernie wisely thought it
would give us a little experience in the competitive world of variety
shows. "Go, go!" Bernie kept saying. I asked Gail, "Does he really
think it's a good idea? Or does he just want us out of his hair for a
while?"

Variety, the show business daily, used to have celebrity destination
lists, designating "NY TO LA," "LA TO NY," "LON TO NY," and
one day, we saw ourselves on the "NY TO LA" list . . . Oh My God!
Sinatra's name was on those lists. Doris Day, Cary Grant, you name

it. "Who the hell were Kenny Solms and Gail Parent?" we asked ourselves. And leaving our beloved New York? Our friends? Our family? It was an easy decision. Screw the family. Screw the friends. We were about to make bigger ones in L.A.

Suddenly, I was twenty-four and Carol Burnett was flying me out to L.A. to write a big TV show. I'll never forget it. It was Passover. Joan Rivers arranged to have the airline give us matzoh ball soup. We knew hardly anyone in LA, so we called the only other comedy writer we knew, our friend Treva Silverman. We told her we felt a little homesick, it being Seder night. I'll never forget her reaction. "Fuck Seder," she said calmly. I wonder to this day: how do you fuck a Seder?

When we arrived, Bernie, thank God, met us at the airport. He too was a brand-new resident and hardly knew his way around. "I wonder which way is Hollywood," Bernie wondered, as he had gotten completely lost on the freeway. By the time we arrived at the Sunset Marquis, a kind of halfway house for all the New York exiles, we knew we had made it . . . halfway.

We had to get cars and places to live in LA. Who knew from buying cars and renting houses? We weren't making any real money yet, so we leased them. I knew I couldn't buy a house, but for a couple of hundred dollars a month you could rent furnished homes. I picked a cute two-bedroom mountainside house on Laurel Canyon.

Gail chose a house in Hollywood. It was more sensible, and she had a family to raise. I was a single guy, so I picked a wild, two bedroom pole house on stilts in Laurel Canyon. "Is a Jew in a pole house in Laurel Canyon a funny thing to be?" my New York friends kept asking. I thought so. One-lane hillside roads curving up a mountain, fire hazards threatening you all the way, and living in a house with nothing beneath it. It was a dream world. Gorgeous weather. Gorgeous people. I had neighbors like Joni Mitchell and Dustin Hoffman. What were they doing there? What was I doing there? I knew from nothing. I was still getting checks from my parents for socks and underwear.

It was all so unreal I even remember screaming out the window to a dumbstruck Joni once, "Hey Joni, did you see what happened on Fairfax? They paved paradise and put up a parking lot!" I was insane. She looked at me strangely and never spoke to me again. Can you blame her? I never even saw Dustin Hoffman, but I enjoyed *The Graduate*. Mama Cass was a neighbor too. I knew her from New York so I was less crazy. She was even the one who had helped me find a place. "Just drive around, look for signs," she told me. No, she didn't tell me this on a "Monday, Monday."

Steve Allen had been one of our idols as well. He was even better in real life. A total perfectionist. And that laugh of his was genuine. He cackled all the time. He was everyone's biggest fan and a real cheerleader. He also was one of those memo guys. We received at least two or three of them a day, always reminding us that his wife, Jayne Meadows, should be in every sketch. My favorite sketch was "The Prickly Heat Telethon," where, instead of making money, the tote board kept getting lower. I remember soon-to-be *Laugh-In*'s Ruth Buzzi as the Tote Board Gal pointing to it, still smiling as the amount on the board sank lower and lower. Steve even put me in the sketch where I played the always-scratching "Prickly Heat Poster Boy." Jayne was especially hilarious, playing a huge star singing for her favorite charity a torch song, "Never Forget to Forget Me."

Besides the sketch, I remember something hilarious that night. For my cameo, they put me in a tiny dressing room in the hallway, with just room enough for me. But, as ever, I couldn't resist the "bit." I pretended I was a huge star and rented a piano, bass, and drums, squeezing all of it into this tiny space. I also shoved waiters in there serving canapés and drinks. Steve and Jayne roared. I soon learned a valuable lesson: the broader the bit, the funnier.

Steve and Jayne did their best to introduce us to the Hollywood

Kenny with Steve Allen and Jayne Meadows

scene. Jayne would call, "Kenny, darling, get over here ASAP. Anyone who's anyone is here at the house." They had parties where they jumped, fully clothed, into the pool. Catered lunches. Limousines at our disposal. And this show introduced us to "the room." Essentially "the room" threw five comedy writers into the same space and whoever was loudest would get most of their jokes on the show. They were all older than we were but hilarious and nurturing—except for the Head Writer, a competitive power-grabbing egomaniac. He had the biggest weapon—the typewriter. We just sat around his desk throwing lines. In those days, you only knew you got a line in if you could see him type it. He was a little jealous that Gail and I had already gotten Burnett, the big show of the fall, so our lines would usually fall on deaf ears, no matter how loud we were. It way preceded the days of the computer. It even preceded carbon copies. The Head Writer would do all the typing and literally patch the sketches together with scotch tape and scissors, inserting his favorite bits (usually his own) into the script as if it were a giant puzzle. Then his secretary would do her best to type it up, with him constantly leaning over her shoulder. Ironically, when the series finished, his career went into oblivion, I forget all about him, while all the other writers in the room soared to big success.

A big lesson Gail and I found was how to work with other writers besides ourselves. It had always been the two of us, but then there were other voices. Not only did you learn to listen, you learned to respect. It wasn't just about us anymore. Other people had voices. Some had funnier lines, some had less funny lines, but you were all in it together. There was no room for ego or negativity. The result was what mattered. Mind you, you were dealing with big egos too. Most comedy writers are desperate for that big laugh. But when you all had that common goal, that's what rose above everything. Our group was the same, and when the show ended it was like saying goodbye to bunkmates at camp, friends from high school. You really do get involved.

In this case, one went to Dean Martin, another went to *Laugh-In*, and we went to Burnett. God only knows where that egomaniac Head Writer went. But you learn grace, you learn maturity, and you don't name names. Gary Belkin. B-E-L-K-I-N. Not that I'm still bitter. Of course I am. He once said to Gail and me, "Your agent oversold you." That really hurt Gail's feelings. I was already numb to him, but with just enough strength to put him down every chance I could. Oh, relax—he's long gone. No, it wasn't murder.

THE
CAROL BURNETT SHOW

The good news was we were finally away from him and doing *The Carol Burnett Show.* "So what's Television City like?" my parents asked. While it sounded so glamorous, I had to tell them the truth. It was at the corner of bland Beverly Boulevard and dumpy Fairfax Avenue, next to the filthy Farmers' Market. Yet, you felt like you were at the center of the whole fabulous Hollywood thing.

Luckily we lived only ten minutes from CBS. This job was clearly not a nine-to-fiver. Since we were the youngest on the staff, we were usually there from ten a.m. till midnight and beyond. We were so green. What did we know about rewrites? What the hell were they? We thought it was all perfect the first time. We were pretty naïve but raring to go. I'm not sure everybody else was.

When we signed onto Burnett, I'd love to say everyone around us was going out of their minds and as excited as we were. Sadly, this wasn't true. This was business. We were the only ones encouraged. In fact, our William Morris agent at the time, David Geffen (that's right, *mogul* David Geffen) structured a sliding scale *down* contract. He was trying to out-clever the show's producer, Joe Hamilton. He wanted to be sure we got more money upfront, since no one had faith in the show. Carol had come off a flop and nobody was that excited. I'll never forget the bulletin board story. In those days, scheduling shows was a little more casual—you know, not as many pilots, no upfront publicity, no startup conventions. One day, we were all in the office of Mike Dann, CBS's head of programming, talking about the show. Behind him on a huge bulletin board was a mass of three-by-five cards showing the year's schedule. I startled Carol and Joe by saying, "There's a question mark about our show past January." Dann glared at me. Can you imagine? CBS wasn't sure of our future. Needless to say, nowadays they have locked doors on those boards and huge secrecy about the new season's schedules.

Our head writer, Arnie Rosen, was a tough taskmaster. He had written for variety shows for years, so if anyone knew the drill it was Arnie. Luckily, he got a kick out of us and was very kind . . . for a while. He was under pressure to get a script out every week. He had no time for Kenny and Gail bits and small talk. We quickly made the adjustment and worked like hell to please him, which wasn't easy. Punching up the script, adding jokes, deleting what wasn't working in rehearsal. You had to be quick on your feet. We weren't used to that kind of pressure. "Come up with a funnier joke," Arnie would say nonchalantly. It was easy for him. He had all those years writing for Milton Berle, Phil Silvers, *Get Smart*, huge shows and huge specials. He was in his late fifties, and we were known as "the kids." What did we know? We didn't even have a window in our office, so Arnie drew a picture of one. He made us learn fast.

Working late into the night was like detention hall with laughs. "Arnie, do you mind if I go to the bathroom?" "If you don't mind having an unfunny script," he sassed back. We might not have dragged ourselves out of there until midnight, but we were energetic the next morning. The show wasn't going to air for another month, but it was like planning a big party. Anticipation and frenzy were in the air.

It was clear from the beginning that we would have to adjust our comedy gears for the Burnett show. We started our career with more biting satire such as the "Upstairs" sketches and, of course, the album.

Carol's comedy was more broad-based. The ones famous for their political satire were our neighbors across the hall, the Smothers Brothers. Ironically, because of it they were eventually cancelled. On Burnett, we kind of sneaked in more biting material. Nobody would think that their "dear sweet Carol" could ever get a punch or a jab in there, but we occasionally did. The censors weren't worried about us, so Carol loved it when we fooled them. One sketch in particular was a takeoff on a paid political ad by the president and the first family. Harvey Korman played the frozen and constantly smiling president, who kept waving to America. Carol, the stilted First Lady, proudly mentioned that she was thirty-four point seven years old, "the exact same age of our very *first* First Lady, Martha Washington." Also onstage was an ancient grandmother who was half asleep, a cadet standing rigidly at attention and Minerva, a nervous black maid who accidentally walked onstage asking the president if he wanted his regular prune juice. That's when Carol and Harvey stiffly overreacted and hugged maid Minerva saying that, she was just like one of the family. Minerva retorted nastily with, "Except I sleeps in the basement." Carol and Harvey reacted dumbstruck.

Besides our regulars—Harvey Korman, Vicki Lawrence, Lyle Waggoner—the guests were amazing. We were working with stars ranging from Betty Grable to Lucille Ball, Sid Caesar to Lana Turner, Rita Hayworth to Gloria Swanson, Steve to Eydie. You name it! What a change in my life. Where it was once enough for me to do "bits" for myself, I was now writing "bits" for all these famous people. The more, the merrier, huh? And if I couldn't do the bits myself, then at least I was writing them for a pretty fabulous crowd.

And of course, there was Carol. She was indomitable. Such confidence. Such talent. And so nice. Television doesn't lie. Stars like Carol come right into your living room. She was exactly the way you'd think she'd be. Humble, gracious, and American as apple pie. We hit it off immediately, even though I was as American as rugalah.

Carol and Joe were like a second family to me. "Oh, give me a break," you're thinking, but it was true. I was new in town. I didn't know anyone. In the beginning all I knew was the show. While the socks and underwear were still coming from Philadelphia, I mainly got to hang out with Carol and her kid sister, Christine, who also lived in Laurel Canyon. Carol's kids were adorable. While it was just Carrie and Jody at the time, Erin was born the next year. Joe was very funny and loved putting me on. Since he always thought of me as the gullible kid, I believed everything he said and took it all very literally. There was barely a night when Carol and Joe didn't build up some huge story that I always believed. "You know this house in Beverly

Gail and Joe and Carol and Kenny

Hills didn't cost us a cent. Some workers found ancient stones on the grounds which garnered us a fortune," Joe boasted. I was so green that I accepted that Beverly Hills was an ancient place. I believed every story—lock, stock and barrel. They once tried to convince me that they had six homes across the country. I don't know why I believed the chalet in Aspen. Carol was the most un-athletic person I have ever known and the last person to venture downhill on a snowy mountaintop. But they got me every time. I would do anything to make them laugh, and they didn't mind seeing the bits on paper too.

I remember my parents coming out to see the show in LA. They passed on staying at my rustic pole house and were perfectly fine ensconced at the elegant Beverly Hills Hotel. The big deal on that trip was my mother meeting Carol. We went to La Scala for dinner, and when I introduced her to my mother, her first question to Carol was, "So, what's with Cher?" As if Carol knew everyone and everything that was going on in the entire town. Like Carol was the president of Show Business. Carol screamed with laughter and said supportively, "Now I see where Kenny gets his humor."

My father was less supportive. He interjected immediately, "You should meet his brother Steven. He's the funny one." Carol even put me on the actual show doing "bits" here and there.

That's when the folks in Philadelphia started watching the show regularly. My parents liked the fact that their friends saw me on television. Suddenly, my father was glad I had gone into show business. He wasn't stage-struck. He was like any father, glad that I had steady job. He would have been glad if I had gone into frozen foods. Anything regular. But of course the whole family became critics. "Tell your friend Carol to stop doing that Tarzan thing. It's not funny," complained my Uncle Stanley.

When we began taping the show, the energy was palpable. It had the feeling of live theatre, and seeing it happen right in front of your eyes was more than exciting. We taped two shows—a dress rehearsal and an air show. Then they'd edit between the two. Carol's dressing room was right off the writers' room, so she'd have to pass us after each sketch. I'll never forget the night we first did "As The Stomach Turns," a soap opera take-off. It had gone very well at the dress rehearsal, and as Carol whisked by, half-dressed, she winked at us and said, "We'll be doing that as a department." That's when you go back and do a sketch again and again. You know, each time with a different twist. And we did. That's how departments on variety shows are created. You can't really plan them. It just depends on how they work out the first time and "As The Stomach Turns" was a winner from the beginning.

Our schedule was like a dream. Read a script on Monday, start rehearsal on Tuesday, Wednesday a run-through, Thursday a rehearsal with cameras, and then Friday the two live shows. Naturally, Carol got along great with everybody. Too bad the same couldn't be said about Harvey Korman. It seems he had been rude to one of our guests, Petula Clark. It really rankled Carol. After the show, she marched up those stairs to Harvey's dressing room and told him not to come back on Monday unless he apologized and wore a smile on his face. On Monday, he was grinning ear to ear until Carol told him to wipe that God-awful stupid smile off his face.

Vicki and Lyle were never problems. Lyle was a brilliant businessman who was always thinking of making money. He started his own fan club. He would also charge fans for pictures. More for buttons. Years later, he became phenomenally successful selling "Star Waggons," huge portable dressing rooms that are now used on location for moviemaking.

Vicki was clever too. When the word got out that we were looking for someone to play Carol's sister in a segment called "Carol And Sis," she wrote to Carol and invited her to see her perform in her high school musical. Carol and Joe rushed to see it, and eventually she was tested and won the role. Of the questions Carol has been asked all these years, the most popular is: Is Vicki Lawrence your sister? No she isn't, but she sure did look like her. To this day, I still do that bit to Carol, asking her constantly if Vicki Lawrence is her sister. Carol always says the same thing, "No, she isn't, and that's all the time we have for questions and answers." Anything to shut me up. She loves doing bits with me. While her fame is for being a hilarious comedian, few people know Carol has a funny and racy side, like my other gal pal, the late Joan Rivers did. Carol is as fast as they come, too, and can improvise with the best of them. Once we were doing a takeoff on MGM musicals. Unbeknownst to Carol, while she was belting out a Judy Garland song downstage, upstage a horse was "taking care of his business" so to speak. The audience was beyond itself laughing in true hysterics. When Carol finally caught what was going on, she ad-libbed to the musical director Pete Matz, "Pete, do you want to take it from number one or number two?"

I loved making appearances on the show. Once I was cast as Vicki's husband on a takeoff of *The Newlywed Game*. Vicki decided to play the wife character as an over-the-top ditz. I played her goofy Nehru-suited husband. She came up with a fabulous dumb giggle that got more laughs from the audience then any line in the sketch. That was the first time we all discovered Vicki was quite a funny lady in her own right. Eventually, that laugh invaded other sketches, leading to her penultimate performance as Mama in "Mama's Family." Writers Dick Clair and Jenna McMahon created those classic characters. Dick was a huge believer and investor in cryonics, the low-temperature preservation of dead bodies, a procedure he would eventually partake in. And while I'll always remember Eunice and Mama screaming their lungs out, why is the image of Dick chilling in an icebox somewhere in the valley a more hysterical image?

Relationships were building. It was like a family. Joe's secretary dumped her husband to marry one of the stage managers. Then years later she dumped the stage manager for Tim Conway. It was as if the show had its own "As the Stomach Turns."

Kenny with Vicki Lawrence, in my Nehru suit

I was the lone person on the show playing the singles scene. In Hollywood, I would go to the famed Factory and frug the night away. I even did the Studio 54 scene in New York. Nobody knew who I was, but I acted as if I was famous and tagged along with people like Jill Haworth and my friend Sal Mineo.

Around now, you might be thinking, "What a life this guy has." Young, single, working on a hit show, living in a big house, driving a fancy car, hanging out with celebrities day and night. Well, was he happy, you might wonder? A little.

While I admit I had always wanted to be famous myself, I could soon see that, when fame touched some of my famous friends, it wasn't always so fabulous. Interrupting you at dinner was a drag, stopping you in the street was rude. I came to prefer the insulation of not being the one who gets bothered or touched. It's almost like being a celebrity to the celebrities. That was a step above the crowd. I always admired how Carol was with her fans. When anyone approached her for an autograph, she always asked for the person's name. That somehow relaxed the fan and put the two of them on an even keel. And no, there were no under-the-breath cynical comments like, "Out of my way, asshole." She saved those for me.

While Carol was always sweet to fans, Lauren Bacall was her counterpoint. I was coming out of a stage door with her one night and when throngs begged for her autograph she rejected pieces of paper and said, "Playbills only," as we zoomed off into the night. The late Bacall was just one of my famous friends I could namedrop. Over the years I've met so many, yet I didn't want this to be one of those namedropping books. Cher.

I always looked forward to Wednesdays. That's when all the writers, the prop people, the costumes, the hair and make-up people, and the stage managers would watch a run-through in a bare rehearsal hall. No sets. No costumes. Just bare bones. Now Carol always knew I loved Ethel Merman. She was another idol. Ever since I saw her in *Gypsy* when it was trying out in Philadelphia, I had adored her. Talk about second-acting. I must have seen that show twenty-five and a half times. It's how I learned to strip.

Anyway, here we are, years later, and Ethel Merman is on our show! "I can't believe Merman is on our show," I would gush to Carol. Me, the kid from Philadelphia who used to hang out at the Shubert Theatre stage door just to get a quick peek at her. I made up my mind I was going to see her closer than anyone else in that room. Of course, that's what I thought. Unfortunately, that day Ethel didn't yet seem to know all the lyrics of her song and, who knows, maybe her eyes were starting to go a bit. All I know is I never did see Ethel Merman's face that day. The huge cue cards were slammed right in front of her so she could see the lyrics but I couldn't see her. Of course, I heard her. Who couldn't? You could hear her in Cleveland. And of course, Carol kept looking at me, laughing, absolutely hysterical that I couldn't really see Ethel anyway. Here I was so close to my Merman but we had no contact whatsoever.

Maybe it was just as well. That day, for some reason, Merman wasn't singing any of her classics, like, "Everything's Coming Up Roses" or "There's No Business Like Show Business." Nope. That day she decided to belt out Glen Campbell's "Gentle On My Mind." Who would have thought? Ethel Merman goes country!

ETHEL (à la Merman)

AND IT'S KNOWING I'M NOT SHACKLED
BY FORGOTTEN WORDS AND BONDS
AND THE INK STAINS THAT HAVE DRIED UPON
    SOME LINE
THAT KEEPS YOU IN THE BACKROADS
BY THE RIVERS OF MY MEM'RY
THAT KEEPS YOU EVER GENTLE ON MY MIND.

THOUGH THE WHEAT FIELDS AND THE CLOTHES
    LINES
AND THE JUNKYARDS AND THE HIGHWAYS COME
    BETWEEN US
AND SOME OTHER WOMAN CRYING TO HER
    MOTHER
'CAUSE SHE TURNED AND I WAS GONE . . .

My Ethel. Barely a word between us the entire week. I couldn't look at her for the rest of the week. Years later, I was producing a special called *Texaco's Star Theatre Celebrates America's Greatest Musicals . . . 23*

Show-Stopping Songs in a 90-Minute Special. Catchy title, huh? Anyway, she was one of the guest stars, and I was one of the producers. I asked her out to dinner. She growled at me, "Honey, do you know any joint where I can get a nice thick steak?" She was very delicate that way. What a meal. I kept sitting there throwing lines at her like, "We're still stuck with that wind machine you got to blow my clothes off." Nothing registered. I persisted. "You read book reviews like they were books." Nothing. "I made her and now I can make you."

She finally said as she wiped the ketchup off her face, "Honey, what the hell are you talking about?"

I replied, "Ethel, all these lines are from *Gypsy.* The greatest show lines ever written."

She said, "Honey, once I close a show, it all goes right out of my head."

I'll always have Merman on my mind and the memory of the ketchup on her face.

Ethel and Carol

TIM CONWAY

O h, those Burnett shows. You never knew what was going to happen, especially when Tim Conway joined the show as a regular. He always did a solo spot but he had to furnish that material himself. It wasn't written by the staff. He liked Gail and me, so he hired us to write those bits. The first one we wrote for him was called "The Dentist." The premise was very simple: a dentist's first day in the office. You know, a young nervous doctor, being overly attentive to Harvey Korman, his first patient. Funny, but nothing to die from until Tim got his hands on it.

He always did the same thing. In the first show, the dress rehearsal, he would do the sketch exactly as written. Very funny, but just what was written on the page. Then there was the air show. He'd save up all the surprises for that one. Well, on this particular night he was especially geared up. Harvey was giggling from the beginning of the sketch at Tim's antics. Carol was screaming from the wings. The giggles turned into breaking up when Tim decided to take no prisoners that night. The novocaine needle that he jabbed into his hand made his arm frozen, swatting bees and dangling it in front of Harvey's hysterically laughing face. In fact, Harvey started screaming with tears in his eyes, especially when the needle now hit Tim's *leg*, forcing him to limp through the rest of the sketch. The audience was going out of their minds, shrieking with laughter. And when Tim stuck the needle into his forehead, it was the longest laugh I had heard since starting the show. Some argue that the laugh in "Went with the Wind," our spoof on "Gone With the Wind," had a longer laugh. I'm not sure. However, what I am sure of is that our famous and hilarious costume designer, Bob Mackie, might have indeed put a curtain rod on Carol's shoulders as she made her descent down the stairs to greet Harvey Korman's Captain Rat Butler, but he didn't write the now infamous line, "I saw it in the window and I just couldn't resist it." I should know, because I didn't write the line either. Not that I don't take credit for it, if asked. I do take credit for knowing that "The Dentist" sketch is shown at most dental schools across the country. I wish I could get residuals for that, or at least a free filling or two.

One sour note about the dentist. Performers as brilliant as Tim and Carol do not love to talk about writers too much. They want the audience to think whatever comes out of their mouths is their own doing at the very moment it happens. It still galls me, to this day, when Tim and Carol take credit for sketches like "The Dentist." While Gail and I wrote the sketch, including stabbing his hand with novocaine, you'd never know it from their appearances on talk and clip shows. Last week, I even heard Carol say that Tim's dentist sketch should be put in a time capsule. I mentioned to Tim and Carol their misperceptions about this sketch several times, but to no avail. Well, at least now it's in print. WE wrote the dentist sketch. The proof on the next page.

Speaking of bits, nobody did more than Tim onstage and off. I couldn't keep up with him. Tim never stopped this process of ad libbing and breaking everyone up on the air show. During the entire series, Carol and everybody else were very professional and stuck to the script as written. With Tim, you didn't want to. Everyone looked forward to his antics. The first time he did the "old man" character, he shuffled across the stage so slowly, taking forever just to squeeze every laugh from the audience. And he always succeeded. Talk about "stopping the show," there wasn't a week that he didn't. One of my

"THE DENTIST" (CONT'D)

          TIM (CONT'D)
...take a hold of tooth...

          HARVEY
Look, if it's going to hurt, give
me something to kill the pain.

          TIM
Right. Let's see, that would
be novocaine.

(TAKES OUT NEEDLE AND GIVES IT TO
HARVEY TO HOLD WHILE HE READS)
Here, hold this while I see how
it works.

(READS AND GRABS FOR NEEDLE AT SAME TIME)
Take solid hold of hypodermic needle.

(STABS HIMSELF)

Oh... ah... boy. That hurts...
(HAND GOES LIMP)

Well, let's have a go at it.
(CAN'T PICK UP PLIERS, CAN'T GET HIS
HAND IN HIS MOUTH. SWATS FLY WITH
HIS LIMP HAND)

I think I see it.
(TIM PULLS DOWN LIGHT AND IT HITS
HARVEY IN THE FACE)

          HARVEY
(MOANING)

Ahhh!

(HARVEY PULLS OUT HIS OWN TOOTH HIMSELF)

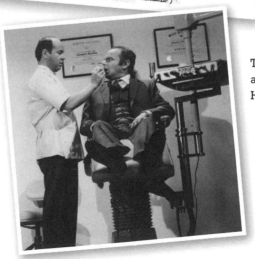

Tim
and
Harvey

favorite memories is of Tim being returned from cold storage delivery on a rack, hanging as the old man.

One of his least favorite moments was I when I visited him in his hometown of Chagrin Falls, Ohio. I would do anything to make Tim laugh. My exit off the plane was a good bit to make this happen. I was wearing yet another Nehru suit in this ramshackle town. Tim died when he ran into his old football coach at the airport and had to introduce me, this theatrical character, to his good ol' buddy boy. Tim's parents had no idea that Tim was funny or that they were funny. When I visited their home, his mother boasted that it was one of the oldest houses in Ohio and showed me a picture-book immortalizing this. Tim later told me that she'd been checking the book out from the local library for the last ten years and would continue to do so until her dying day. Checking it in and out and in and out was just fine for her. She refused to buy the book, since the library owned a copy already, even though most of the time it stayed in her own house. Tim knew I would die from this, and we continue to laugh about it till this day. As far as bits go, Tim has outdone me. He once flew from LA to Washington, D.C., where Carol was performing in *I Do, I Do*, just to hand her a prop when she came offstage. As he handed her the prop, he just smiled a hello and went on his way back to the airport. Another time, in Hawaii, Carol and Joe were having dinner on a veranda, and Tim climbed down from a huge palm tree to join them. He'll do anything for a laugh. Why do I relate to these people? Because I do the same thing. Bits! Bits! Bits!

However, it can turn on you. Just last week I made a fool of myself at a party where one of the guests was in a wheelchair. The host and all his friends were making a big deal about how they could get their friend down to the main level. I whispered, "Why doesn't he just get out of the chair and walk down?" The host was not amused.

BITS

In high school, a "bit" cost me money. It was pouring rain in Philadelphia, and I was driving my date home. I didn't want her to get wet, so I insisted on dropping her at her front door. Unfortunately, her front door was thirty feet down a hill. Nobody in his right mind would have driven down that hill, rain or no rain. Well, I zoomed right down it, constantly saying to her, "No, I insist. I'll drop you off at the front door." Well, it was a debacle. The car needed to be towed out. Their lawn was ruined, and I had to pay for all the damages. Sometimes these things take you over, and nothing will stop you doing the "bit." Of course, there are consequences for this behavior, but it's like a demon inside you that you can't resist. I often hear critical comments like, "Kenny, you've gone too far this time." I can never think of going far enough. It can win some fans but make a few enemies along the way, especially in the rain.

Carol is the same way. When she was a kid living off Hollywood Boulevard, she and her grandmother used to see at least two movies a day. That began her love of the Silver Screen. She even worked as an usher at the old Warner Theatre on Hollywood Boulevard until that fateful day she was fired for not allowing a couple in to see the ending of Alfred Hitchcock's *Strangers on a Train*. She just loved the movie too much to ruin it for anybody. The manager saw it another way. She must still have traumatic memories of that day he tore off the epaulets of her uniform, railing at her, "You're never gonna make it in show business." He really showed her, didn't he?

Carol never soured on the movies. In fact, she was rare and ready to spoof all her idols when she got her own television show. I was lucky enough to write some of them. Our "Gilda," which we called "Golda," was a classic. Rita Hayworth even wrote her a fan letter and Carol invited her to be a guest on the show. When Carol played Doris Day, she carried a heavy suitcase. "Extra freckles," she explained. When she played Joan Crawford, she had one eyebrow going across her face, not to mention shoulder pads as high as Crawford's beehive hair.

Crawford adored Carol. In fact, one night at New York's fashionable Four Seasons Restaurant, Joan wouldn't leave Carol alone. When Crawford spotted her across the room, she couldn't stop blowing kisses Carol's way and staring at her the whole time. About twenty minutes later she was much closer. She had gotten on her knees and her head was literally next to Carol's plate. How they got Ms. Crawford up and out of there I don't know, but it's an unforgettable image.

Carol's Esther Williams topped them all. We actually went to Carol's house and filmed her in the pool. Yes, she sang underwater, hit her head on the side, and dove upwards back into her room, while towel-drying her head, revealing in an instant a huge mane of hair. Ricardo Montalban serenaded a waterlogged "Esther" with "Baby, It's Cold Outside," drenching himself every time he touched her. What a thrill it was for the star-struck Carol to have all these stars on her very own show.

One night it backfired. It happened very early in her career, when she and Joe lived in the same building in New York as author John Steinbeck. One day, he got in the elevator and Carol froze. He broke the silence by raving about Carol's weekly performance on Garry Moore. "I hope you don't mind my telling you what a big fan I am," Steinbeck enthused. She couldn't believe *the* John Steinbeck was talking to her or that he knew who she even was. She was so startled that, when he got off the elevator at his floor, she introduced her husband Joe as "Frank," just as the door was closing. Joe wouldn't speak to her for the rest of the evening. She forgot her husband's name.

While the Burnett show kept going strong, with us losing money each week thanks to Mogul David Geffen's great deal, we still earned enough to start buying houses and cars. What did we know from buying houses? We thought escrow was a summer camp. I bought my first house from Michael Wilding and Margaret Leighton. It was famous because Michael Wilding owned it when he was married to Elizabeth Taylor. It was across the street from Liberace's house. Every real estate deal in Hollywood was somehow connected to a celebrity, whether they lived there or not.

Years later, when I actually met Elizabeth, she was doing an HBO movie with Carol in Canada. Carol asked me to co-host a birthday party honoring Elizabeth's fiftieth. She was everything you've heard

Kenny with Elizabeth Taylor

about and more. Her laugh was legendary, and I loved that I got a big one out of her. For her birthday, I gave her a check for twenty-five dollars and wrote in the memo section, "Birthday Present for Elizabeth Taylor." She roared with laughter and cashed the check.

THE BUZZ

It was the seventies. Long hair, Nehru suits, bell bottoms. All very Hollywood. Parties. Pools. Pool parties. Pot. Pot pool parties. All that neon flashing in your face. The whole deal. That's when the friends from Philadelphia and family would visit. "You've changed," they would like to say. I hadn't remotely changed. They were the judgmental ones. My first car wasn't too pretentious: a blue Cadillac convertible, the one with the fins. I played down the next car. It was a used Mercedes, but once used by Jackie Gleason. Too bad it came with a gear shift. Being from the east coast and Jewish, I could only drive automatic and burned out the gear shift within a week.

Parents coming to L.A. for visits were always an event. One year, I somehow got my parents tickets to the Oscars. An impossible task. It was the year Charlie Chaplin returned to Hollywood. A big event. But not for my parents. They didn't like their seats. "I could see it better at home," my father growled.

My father was never really thrilled about my success. He thought show business was for lowlifes. Nice. He thought his son was a deadbeat. Getting out of limos, winning awards, nothing changed his mind. I didn't realize until years later that he was right. Years later when I wasn't as "hot," I noticed the lowlifes were everywhere, but I adjusted. True, agents didn't call you back, producers ignored you, headwaiters now sat you in the back of the room near the kitchen, but it didn't really matter. That became subjective, a harmless thing that just happens in this town. When you understand it, you don't take it that seriously. It comes with the turf. It's a vanity-oriented profession, very much the "hot today, cold tomorrow" mentality. If you don't accept it you can easily fall victim to it, but it's not worth it. It's superficial.

It was a time of Hollywood excess, but not for us. We were too busy working. A great schedule. We'd get weeks off at a time, but we always worked during them. We'd do specials, sitcoms, and even one of those new ABC Movies of the Week: *Call Her Mom*. It starred Connie Stevens as a housemother at a frat house. It was one of the highest rated movies on ABC and a precursor of the film *Animal House*. During any time we had off from Burnett, we would write situation comedy episodes for *The Mary Tyler Moore Show*, *All In The Family*, *The Bill Cosby Show*, and our own pilot starring our beloved Tim Conway. Tim did so many pilots he had a license plate that said "13 WKS." That's how long ours ran.

Summer shows were a thing of the day. I already mentioned Steve Allen, but a lot of stars had them: Sonny and Cher, Flip Wilson, Glen Campbell, Jimmy Rogers, The Fifth Dimension, Shields and Yarnell. They were mimes. Do you hate anything more in the world? What about their parents' reaction? "Mom, Dad, I want to become a mime." CBS's cafeteria was like a Hollywood studio commissary. Stars of all the shows, the guests, all the writers, Martha Raye walking around in Vietnam fatigues with a sign saying "Fuck Peace." Pretty. The Smothers Brothers also began their career with a summer show on CBS. Years later, we produced a series for them on NBC. That wasn't easy. The boys wanted to be political rather than funny. We saw more of the censors than Tom and Dick.

There was a bit of a buzz surrounding Gail and me. Probably from Gail and me. One of the more embarrassing publicity stunts was surprising Carol on a local talk show, *Keene at Noon*. So humiliating. While Carol was being interviewed, we walked on stage, not only to surprise her, but as if we were big celebrities. Poor Carol had to act surprised. Some surprise. She had just seen us a half-hour before at the office. She was probably wondering why we weren't back there working. Eventually, Gail and I even joined the talk show circuit, from Merv Griffin to Johnny Carson. Not really a circuit. It was just Merv Griffin and Johnny Carson. Our first Carson guest shot was really memorable: we didn't get on. Time had run out. There we were, standing in the wings, in full make-up, hearing Johnny say, "Sorry, we're running over and we couldn't get to Kenny and Gail Solms." That was a surprise. Not only were we not getting on but we were now married. Eventually we were booked again and this time actually got on. We did a spoof on Miss America, and Johnny liked this night-club bit I used to do. I'd play one of those typical sleazy nightclub singers. The kind that Bill Murray did years later on *Saturday Night Live*. How dare he!

KENNY: (Singing) STAND WELL BACK, I'M COMING THROUGH.
(Speaking) Hi. (Singing) NOTHING CAN STOP ME NOW.
(Speaking) Where you from?
(Singing) WATCH OUT WORLD, I'M WARNING YOU.
(Speaking) What's your sign?
(Singing) NOTHING CAN STOP ME NOW!
(Speaking) Stop. You know, ladies and gentlemen if we could just get serious for a moment. If we could just reach out and touch one another. If we could just talk to one another regardless of race, creed or color. But most important of all, ladies and gentlemen . . .
(Singing) IF WE COULD TALK TO THE ANIMALS, JUST IMAGINE IT, CHATTIN' WITH A CHIMPIN' CHIMPANZEE.
(Singing) IMAGINE TALKIN' WITH A TIGER, CHATTIN' WITH A CHEETAH.
WHAT A NEATA ACHIEVEMENT THAT WOULD BE . . .

Johnny laughed a lot, but maybe not that much. We were never booked again.

While Carol would do anything for a laugh in a sketch, I was always up for a bit anytime anywhere. One night my "spontaneity" got us into a little bit of trouble. We were having dinner at Joe Allen's in LA. Out of the blue, I brought up the movie version of *Annie*. The rights had been purchased by Columbia, and it was no secret around town that producer Ray Stark and director John Huston wanted Carol to play Miss Hannigan. Too bad she didn't want to. In fact, she sort of shrugged it off. She had never even seen the show. "You've never seen the show!? You'd be a shoo-in for an Oscar," I said. "I know what we're going to do," I added, as I swiftly finished my burger, determined to get on the move. "It's playing here. We're going to the Shubert right now. We'll at least catch the second act." Carol hadn't even finished her salad, and she kept protesting and saying, "It's too late. They're in the middle of the show." Who did she think she was talking to? Nothing ever stopped me from getting into a show before. So we hightailed it over there, Carol protesting but laughing all the way.

While I must admit that, though all the sealed glass doors of this modern theatre seemed daunting, I knew I'd find a way in. In New York, there was always a door open somewhere. Carol kept saying, "Kenny! No! No!" I kept saying, "Yes, yes, yes! It'll be a snap."

I peered into the lobby and there was nobody in sight. No usher. No manager. Nothing. Obviously, intermission was over. I tapped on the door. Carol was mortified. Finally, an usher came to the door. She couldn't have been more than sixteen. "Can I see your ticket, please?" Before she could stop us, we were speeding into the theatre as if I owned the place. We headed for the balcony. It was half-empty and we tiptoed in.

This was so exciting. Carol was about to see the reprise of "Easy Street," the show-stopping number from the first act. Well, at least I hoped she would. Unfortunately, the teenage usher had caught up with us. I had to think fast on my feet saying, "I'm Ray Stark and I just bought this show for ten million dollars. I want Carol here to get a peek at it." This girl had no idea what I was talking about. She had no idea who Ray Stark was and didn't even look at Carol. Oh my God. Was I going to fail? Ray Stark would have died for Carol to get a glimpse of the show, even though Carol wasn't interested. Neither was the usher. She didn't want to see a contract. She just wanted to see a stub. Carol had one hand covering her face while the other was stabbing me in the ribs. We had no choice but to flee the scene. We were out of that theatre and into the parking lot before "Easy Street" even began. But that didn't stop me. I had the cassette in the car and belted out the number along with it, which made Carol even more hysterical.

A few weeks later, I was vacationing with Carol at her home in Hawaii. Her manager, Bill Robinson, was calling from the mainland. Bill told Carol that Ray Stark still wanted her for *Annie*. Laughing it off, Carol shrugged and said kiddingly, "Sure, I'll do it . . . for a million bucks," giggling as she innocently hung up the phone. An hour later, Bill called back. "You got the million," he told her. She was incredulous. She had never made that much money in her entire life. It was like a Hollywood dream. The only bad news was now she *had* to do the movie. I wonder if that usher ever saw it.

We didn't know how good we had it, though. Then again, yes we did. The country was ablaze with demonstrations against the war. We were writing jokes. Everyone else our age was storming Washington. We were going to the Emmys. They were going to jail. We were going to openings.

While the Burnett show sounds like a perfect experience, it wasn't always. In the fourth season, a little competition set in between Arnie and us. We noticed we weren't getting as many sketches on as usual. Arnie was a bit distant as well. "Where are our sketches?" I would ask Gail. "Where's the Joan Crawford takeoff?

The Shelley Winters?" We discovered he had never even shown them to Carol or Joe. While it was his prerogative, it seemed strange. We knew just what Carol would love, and yet there was this mystery. That was solved soon when I discovered most of our sketches in his bottom drawer. Yes, I went snooping. What else is there to do on a Thursday night at eleven o'clock when Arnie went for a bathroom break? Carol indeed loved the sketches. She was furious with Arnie. And Arnie was furious with us. He prevailed, and we weren't invited back for the fifth season. It was a definite jolt, probably the most profound one we had yet received.

It was a strange time. We had never been out of work. We didn't know these winning streaks just continued and that someday you just might be off one. While we picked up odd jobs along the way, it was different. Not going to CBS every day, not getting that steady check.

Joe must have felt guilty. That next season he was executive producing a new *Smothers Brothers Show*, and he hired us to be producers and head writers. He must have meant well, but the experience was a mixed blessing. While it was fun hiring some wonderful writers, including Chevy Chase, Pat Proft, Mickey Rose, and an entirely hilarious squad, Tommy and Dick were very difficult. They were argumentative from the beginning, always looking for that intense and meaningful sketch rather than the funny one. Any political spin was never enough. While the show limped along for thirteen weeks and Chevy would do his best to lighten all our spirits, careening down every stairway he met and ending on his butt, it was not a fun gig until guest star Milton Berle did a hilarious monologue in total drag. What was so wonderful was that he never referred to being dressed as a woman. He delivered a fiery oration on an entirely different subject than crossdressing. The more serious he got on this other subject and never referring to drag, the funnier he got. He was one of those people we were privileged to work with . . . Always fun, always on and always reliable. A total perfectionist. Right down to the last false eyelash.

A year later we were back with Carol again. Thank God. It was a special called *Sills and Burnett at the Met*, taping live from New York City's Lincoln Center. Once again, my parents drove in to New York from Philly. They said the same thing. They weren't that impressed with the Met. "You can see that better on television, too." I thought my brother would be excited sitting there in rehearsal. His kid brother writing there at the Metropolitan Opera! The truth is he couldn't stand sitting, he wanted to get out. He couldn't understand the concept of rehearsal. "Ken, why are they doing it over and over and over again? I'm going out of my mind."

Years later I wrote and produced a special called *Burnett Discovers Domingo*, obviously starring Carol and the fabulous Placido Domingo. Needless to say, I didn't invite them back. I wonder if they were able to take that loss.

On yet another special featuring Placido and Carol, a major "bit" occurred. Although the show itself was quite successful, this one happened offstage. It was a two-hour special, *Texaco Salutes Broadway*, starring a cavalcade of Broadway stars. We thought it would be fun to include Placido Domingo dueting "You're Just In Love" with Carol from Irving Berlin's *Call Me Madam*. Both agreed it would be great fun, but there was a hitch. Placido couldn't fly to LA for the special. That didn't daunt us. Coincidentally, Carol was going to be in London for a few days, where Placido was performing. Our brilliant director, Marty Pasetta, sold Placido and Carol on a way to include them in the show. All he needed was an empty studio in London where he could use a device called "blue screen" and seamlessly include them in the special. There was one more hitch. Since Carol had already done a number on the show, which we had already taped in LA, her outfits had to match. She agreed to do the gig on one condition: that I schlep the ball gown to London. A perfect set-up for a Kenny-Carol

Kenny with Placido

bit. I took the heavy gown to London, walked down the hallway of the hotel we were staying in, and knocked on Carol's door, saying, "I have the gown." She opened the door and needless to say, I was in it. A classic bit. Carol even topped it. Although she was dying inside, she kept a straight face and deadpanned, "Oh, great, Kenny—can you slip that off and hang it in my closet?" I've included the pictures. Who do you think is prettier? What can I say? I'm so glad we had this time together but as Carol always said when she had to move on, "That's all the time we have for questions and answers."

Carol with Placido

Kenny in Carol's gown

SPECIALS

arol wasn't the only one with specials. Week in and week out, everybody had one: Mitzi Gaynor, Shirley MacLaine, Julie Andrews, the Muppets, Bing Crosby, Ann-Margret (I used to call her Ann Hyphen Margret). Hers was called *From Hollywood with Love*. We had gotten Lucille Ball to do the show, and one of the sketches was going to be Ann-Margret and Lucy, dressed as tourists, visiting stars' homes and eventually each other's.

A week before the taping, the producer, Burt Rosen came in and said, "Lucy is not on the show anymore, but don't worry. We can still do the sketch, but it will be with Godfrey Cambridge now." As if everything was interchangeable. That sketch was finally cancelled, thank you. Instead we did something with her and Dean Martin, some ridiculous sketch where they pretended what it would be like being married to each other. You can guess the bits. He drank a lot, she wore a lot of wigs. He was in a tux; she was dressed as a kitten with a whip. Nothing made sense. Nothing was remotely funny. They were just glad to get Dean on the show. Here's the way it worked with all these stars: they'd each do each other's specials. It was about favors, trade-offs. You do my special, I'll do yours. Sort of like my days at NYU, but with stars.

An exception was *The Many Sides of Don Rickles*. With Norman Lear and Bud Yorkin producing, we wrote a sketch called "Midnight Monk," where we had Rickles as Brother Gregory, a shy and unassuming monk whose life is being portrayed in a Hollywood movie starring Robert Goulet as the now gorgeous Brother Gregory. Don Adams played the frenetic director. Of course, poor Brother Gregory's life was all rewritten for the movies, glamorizing it completely, and Rickles had to constantly hold back his temper tantrums and slow burn. Hilarious situation.

Annie And Her Hoods, starring Anne Bancroft, was an Emmy Award-winning special that had clever and edgy material. Our sketch was considered a standout. Under the banner of "unlikelihoods," Bancroft disclosed to a stuffy BBC interviewer, played with relish by Carl Reiner, that Annie, our Jewish princess, was going to marry Prince Charles. She wanted to gut the palace and go to Puerto Rico and the Virgin Islands on their honeymoon. She assumed she owned it anyway. She was also excited to announce she would serve chicken à la king at the reception.

I once did a special I never did. Let me explain. It was for Roseanne. She insisted on doing a Hanukkah special for ABC. ABC didn't know what they were buying and soon became leery about the whole project. A Hanukkah special? Even though all the executives were Jewish, none of them would admit it, and they weren't too keen on the whole project. Roseanne was insistent. She assured me we could do anything we wanted. That was true until ABC got the script. Yes, they pulled it. I was paid *not* to do it. It was called a buyout. I took the money and ran from that one. But I left the yarmulkes.

In the late thirties, Olsen and Johnson's *Hellzapoppin,* was a smash on Broadway. It was a Vaudeville revue which preceded *Rowan and Martin's Laugh-In* by forty years. In the early seventies, Alexander H. Cohen, an eminent Broadway producer, optioned it for a television special. Much like the zany show itself, the writing staff was hilarious and gag-crazy. Luckily, Gail and I were included in the mayhem. Everything was going well except for one problem. We had no Olsen and Johnson. Alex had lists and lists, but no hosts until the day before rehearsal. God knows what we were writing since we didn't know who we were writing for. Not one to worry, Alex kept telling us to just write dialogue for "A" and "B." No personality traits, no styles, no quirks, just A and B or, as Alex kept reminding us, "Call them 'Star A' and 'Star B' if that would help!"

Eventually, Jack Cassidy and Ronnie Schell completed the casting as our Olsen and Johnson. They were irreverent and silly, and, like Vaudeville itself, the show had a freewheeling and anything-goes comedy about it. Blackouts, sketches, funny songs, and a supporting ensemble of up-and-coming comedians. We even had critic Rex Reed in the audience seriously critiquing the show as it went on. His deadpan and sophisticated delivery was a hilarious counterpoint to the mayhem that was going on in front of him. I was in a lot of the sketches, and Gail played a bored yenta in the audience who was not at all amused by the proceedings. It only aired once but you can probably find it on YouTube. Among the guests were the legendary Jackson Five debuting "Got to Be There." Who could know at the time that one of the Five would be destined to be the oddest thing on the show?

LORELEI

When Gail and I got signed for a Broadway show, we couldn't believe it. It was everything I had always dreamed of. Who would have guessed it would end up a nightmare? Alas, here's where the success streak started to slide. The show was called *Lorelei*, and it starred Carol Channing. It was a revisit of *Gentlemen Prefer Blondes*, which she had done twenty years before on Broadway. We had to find a hook why Lorelei was still singing "Diamonds Are a Girl's Best Friend" at the age of eighty.

It was a dream package. Besides Channing, it was Jule Styne's music, and Betty Comden and Adolph Green were going to write new lyrics to enhance Leo Robin's already existing brilliant lyrics. I remember the day we pitched it to Channing. We told her it would be a flashback of Lorelei's life after her husband, Gus, died. I could tell it worked. She lit up and with a big smile said, "He dies!" I still don't know why she thought that was funny. But the important thing is that she liked it. So did Jule. He even started playing "Bye Bye Baby." One hitch: there was no piano in the room. His excited fingers were playing the desk.

That show had a weird schedule. The producers wanted to get their investment back fast, so we were on the road for an entire year before it went to Broadway. About six directors were fired. Miss Channing was not talking to any of the writers. Of course two of them were dead: author Anita Loos and lyricist Leo Robin. To calm things down,

Kenny with Betty and Adolph and Gail

Gail suggested we encourage Channing: "Tell her you liked the tech. Maybe she'd be nicer to us." She was convinced that Channing couldn't actually see us, as her vision wasn't that great. So I went right up to her. "That was a great tech rehearsal," I said. She growled right back at me, "You do your job and I'll do mine." In an instant, Gail turned to me and whispered, "I still don't think she saw you."

Another weirdness on the show was Channing's husband and manager, Charles Lowe. A former Navy captain, Charles was always there. He never missed a performance, and he would always lead the audience in applause and laughter. A very temperamental type, he deserved his reputation for being a pain in the ass. Once in Oklahoma City, where we were opening the show, he stormed onto the stage and screamed at a stagehand who was gluing red carpet down the aisles of the theatre. Lowe was in a rage. "Don't you know Miss Channing is allergic to glue? If you want to have a show tonight, go find yourself another Lorelei," he screamed. The teenage stagehand didn't even notice Charles and continued gluing his way down the aisle. An absurd moment in an absurd show.

I schlepped the parents in for that one too, and my Uncle Stanley. My uncle loved it. He loved Carol Channing. She wasn't talking to us, but he loved her. We got back at her, though. I mean, we didn't *do* anything, but she had egg on her face the night the show opened in LA. She had this prepared speech she would do at the curtain call in every city we played. She would say, "You dear, dear people of Houston and environs, you dear, dear people of Chicago," and so on. But opening night in LA was different. She had just closed in San Francisco, but didn't seem to remember. There she was, downstage center, opening that big mouth to everyone in LA and saying, "You dear, dear people of San Francisco and environs . . . "She forgot where she was.

The show ran for over a year on Broadway, at the Palace. To actually have your name in lights was thrilling, but they didn't shine that long. I should have known Channing was a weird one years ago when she was a guest on the Burnett show. She and Carol did a little station break bit where they played each other. Burnett wore a blonde cloth wig and Channing wore a red one. But there was a problem. Channing said she couldn't do it. She was allergic to red. To the *color* red. I'm still trying to figure that one out. It was cloth. Crazy woman. Very talented but odd. She even brought her own food. Yak meat. The woman smelled. Still smells, and probably still doesn't know where she is.

In all fairness, when she finally divorced Charles Lowe, revealing that he was gay and she had never had sex with him, she became more human and less a stereotype. She stopped wearing the blonde wigs and let her hair grow out. She suddenly became this gray-haired, nice and frank older woman. We even reconnected when I visited backstage at a Jule Styne benefit. I wonder if she remembered me. I still hear Gail's words saying, "I still don't think she saw you."

I wish *Lorelei* had been a more satisfying experience. After all, it was my first really big show on Broadway, a dream I'd always had. But there's no guarantee about what happens in show business. Each new project is a gamble, and I've had my share of success. I also gamble on football games, and I hate losing by a half a point, but what are you going to do? You gotta take the loss. At least *Lorelei* recouped its investment.

SHEILA LEVINE

During the rehearsals of *Lorelei*, Gail and I were busy working on the screenplay of a book she had written, *Sheila Levine Is Dead and Living in New York*. We were literally writing it in the theatre while watching *Lorelei* rehearsals. (Channing must have thought we were sure taking a lot of notes.) Eventually, Paramount bought the script, and we were raring to go. We just needed the star to get the final green light. We were dying to get Barbra Streisand, but so was everybody. That's how this business works. You always start out wanting Barbra Streisand, and you usually end up getting Marilu Henner. We ended up with Elaine May's daughter, Jeannie Berlin, who was so brilliant in *The Heartbreak Kid*. Sidney J. Furie was now attached to the project as director. We were excited, it would be our first feature but, when we started filming, something happened. Ms. Berlin decided she wanted to rewrite every single line and improvise the entire script. The director was obsessed with her and let her do anything she wanted. So there we were. Just like *Lorelei*: thrilled to be there, but seeing it all fall apart.

We weren't terribly surprised. From day one, we were hearing lines we never wrote. We were seeing sets we didn't incorporate. Seeing them was an exaggeration. When we looked at the rushes, we couldn't even make out who was who. Everything Furie shot was done in dark colors. Bob Evans, the head of the studio, agreed. "Could you see anything or was it just me?" he whispered to us.

When they previewed it in New York, it was a little bit like a

Kenny with Danny Thomas

scene out of *Singing in the Rain*. The beginning was promising, and everyone was excited to be there, the book having been a best-seller. As the movie went on, the mood changed, and, by the time the final credits rolled, Gail and I were sitting there hearing comments like, "Oh my God! Why did she do that to her own book?" and "I hated it." I couldn't resist turning to Gail and doing the infamous line from *Singing In The Rain*: "I liked it." Vincent Canby of the *New York Times* sadly said it all: "Something disastrous happened to the heroine of Gail Parent's funny *Sheila Levine is Dead and Living in New York* on her way to the silver screen . . . . This Sheila is so aggressively naïve and dumb, that it's quite impossible to believe that even her family could stand her, to say nothing of the Mr. Right with whom the film provides her." Needless to say, there was no opening night party.

Carol and Joe kindly asked us to come back for the sixth season. I wouldn't have it. I had pride and was $100,000 in debt. I'd show them! Gail went back to the show, and I did not. Much to my dismay, Gail couldn't refuse the offer. She said she needed the money for her family. Well, we had a nice run. After all, we had met in college and had been together for most of our youth. It was like the breakup of a first marriage: too young, too much success. We wanted different things. She wanted more husbands. I wanted to do more things on my own. We're still best friends. In fact we decided to be buried together at Mount Sinai Mortuary. They had a deal going on that we couldn't refuse. One crypt. Head to toe. In perpetuity. Who knows? Maybe we'll collaborate again. We'll have a lot of free time.

Losses are never easy. My life was changing, and I had to go along with it. Without Gail in my life, there was less regularity, less intimacy, and a lot less laughter. A schedule always keeps you busy and helps distract you from the hard realities of the world. I had to reinvent myself. Specials were the way to do it. I had flourished as a producer and a head writer, so it was time to take advantage of the situation.

NOT SO SPECIAL SPECIALS

While Gail eventually went to the world of sitcoms, I stayed in the world of specials, but now I was producing them as well. I met every star. Most were difficult. I'll just do them in bullet points, which is appropriate since, while I was doing them, I wanted to kill myself.

DANNY THOMAS ...
YOUNG AND FOOLISH

I'll never forget the time I had to beg Frank Sinatra to do a Danny Thomas special that was being sponsored by Wendy's. Sinatra wasn't even a guest shot, just a cameo, but it was almost impossible to book him. How do you even get him on the phone? There was no way. But I persevered. I was a producer now. I wanted to prove myself. So I finally tracked him down and got him on the phone. I took a deep breath and asked him if he'd be on the show. "No way, kid," he said. Then he said it again, and again. I persisted. He'd do the show if Dave Thomas from Wendy's would shell out a million dollars to Danny's St. Jude Hospital. Boy, I was suddenly talking big bucks now.

Well, soon came the day of the meeting of the two giants. Me and Sinatra. The day of the taping. Danny wouldn't go to meet him, so I had to meet Mr. Sinatra in the parking lot and guide him into the studio. I was a wreck. "Hi Mr. Sinatra, I'm—." "Yeah, yeah, you got the check, kid?" Very warm. Did Frank sing? Not a note. What, you may ask, did Frank do on the show? Oh, I remember. He left. He got the check from Dave, handed it to Danny, and he was gone. It didn't matter. Danny didn't need the likes of a Frank Sinatra to do his show. He had Barry Manilow and Suzanne Somers join him shimmying to "Copacabana." Not a pretty sight. But Danny felt, that's right: "young and foolish."

TOGETHER AGAIN FOR THE FIRST TIME

This was a Christmas special. This one starred Bing Crosby and Carol Burnett, who were a cleaning crew locked in a department store on Christmas Eve. The most memorable thing that happened on that show didn't happen on stage but off. The crew absconded with about $50,000 worth of store merchandise.

Speaking of jail, my next special took me to Utah and to the Osmonds. It wasn't even Donny and Marie. It was the brothers. And not even Jimmy. Alan! Jay! Merrill! Wayne! Who? It was called:

THE OSMOND BROTHERS: FOUR SPECIALS FOR THE PRICE OF ONE!

We taped it at their studio. I saw Donny and Marie there, but they weren't in the show. You see, when they weren't performing, their parents would make them clean the studio. Nice. Mr. and Mrs. Osmond ignored child labor laws. They managed the kids as well, taking most of their money. Needless to say, that's why Marie is bipolar.

One of the oddest shows I ever did was called:

LEGEND TO LEGEND

Here, one star introduced another star but somehow each was called a legend. Based on the title, it was obvious that the second legend had to be bigger than legend number one. To make the arc of the show work, the first one just had to be just a little less legendary than the second legend. Eventually, we ran out of bona fide legends. By the end of show, Brenda Lee was presenting to Gregory Peck, two people who probably never met and would mostly likely never meet.

While it was a thrill working with all these "legends," the next special was insane.

PLAYBOY'S PAJAMA PARTY AND ROLLERBALL DISCORAMA, PLUS A PREVIEW OF THE PLAYMATE OF THE '80s.

Cute title. Nice and succinct. That was my one pleasure, though. Choosing the Playmate of the '80s. I interviewed each of the beautiful contestants and chose Dorothy Stratten, who a few years later, was tragically murdered by her estranged husband.

We had our production meetings literally on Hugh's bed. Not too distracting, counting bottles of baby oil that were littering the room. I couldn't believe any of us were actually doing this and kept mocking the show as if it would be nominated for an Emmy. "The nominees are, *The Pope: His Holiness Visits the Middle East, Itzak Perlman: Live from Lincoln Center,* and *Playboy's Pajama Party and Rollerball Discorama, Plus a Preview of the Playmate of the '80s.* Hosted by Richard Dawson. Starring Waylon Jennings and Madame." Great night. I was dressed in pajamas, hanging out with puppets.

However, I do remember one funny line that clever Ann Elder wrote. Two playmates were talking to each other. One was bored. "How do you get out of here?" she asked. The other playmate shrugged, "Try turning twenty-one."

LIVE AND IN PERSON

These were three live shows that starred my manager, Sandy Gallin, in a bid to resurrect *The Ed Sullivan Show* of the '50s and '60s. We had every star in the universe, including once again, my old friends the Berosini Orangutans. Joan Rivers guested on that one,

Lily Tomlin

and, while she was there, she fired Sandy. She couldn't understand why he had his own show and she didn't. Kenny Rogers and Dolly Parton did a duet. Siegfried and Roy and Liberace shared a dressing room . . . with the boys from the USC Marching Band. There were wild animals everywhere. Lions, tigers, Rick James . . . The show played three forgettable nights. However, there was one funny bit I loved. I had Lily Tomlin as Ernestine, the switchboard operator, open the top of each show. Ernestine was furious that Sandy had his own show over her. "Why Gallin? I'm just as big a nobody as he is," she barked as she hurled a dart at Sandy's eight-by-ten glossy.

DISNEYLAND'S 30TH ANNIVERSARY CELEBRATION

They may call it the happiest place on Earth. I called it hell. We shot at night and were locked in Disneyland for ten days. Our hosts were John Forsythe and Drew Barrymore. A little problem with one of our hosts. When it came time to shoot, we could never find nine-year-old Drew. Now we know why. She had somehow found a local bar and was throwing back doubles. Nice. No wonder Drew didn't invite her "somehow always missing" mother to either of her weddings. Little Drew was a big drunk.

From the Pointer Sisters to Julie Andrews, stars and fireworks lit up the gorgeous Anaheim skyline. The highlight of this splashy special was the Peter Allen-led finale, "Is There a Band Big Enough?" It was written by fellow Burnett writers Ken and Mitzie Welch. Peter played a *Music Man*-like conductor bringing multitudes of bands to the center of the park from all directions, finally lighting a giant birthday cake. It was a huge production number, directed brilliantly by Marty Pasetta, whom I collaborated with on many specials. Imagine our surprise when little darling Drew popped out of the cake . . . three sheets to the wind.

Even Julian Lennon was on the special. We were all given sharp memos not to approach him or even talk to him because it was too soon after the murder of his father, John.

It was exactly the opposite with Annette Funicello. Because we were late in our shooting schedule we were told to "keep her busy, keep her chatting, keep her occupied, give her food." I'll never forget the stirring dialogue I wrote for Annette there in Disneyland. Here it is:

ANNETTE FUNICELLO: I think everybody wants to live here. But I found something better than living here.

DREW BARRYMORE: You're kidding. What?

ANNETTE FUNICELLO: Coming back. I've been coming back here again and again ever since I was a Mouseketeer.

This special was the first time I ever had to get someone off a show. The network had insisted for some idiotic reason that Sammy Davis be scratched from Disneyland. They were adamant. It couldn't have been racist, but it was just one of those incongruities from network brass to a producer. I was a nervous wreck. Everybody loved Sammy Davis. I had to pitch him an idea I knew he'd hate: I had to make him be the one who didn't want to do the show. What idea would be so pathetic that he'd hate it? Thank God I came up with one. I got him on the phone and asked him what he thought of selling dancing cotton candy to the tourists on Disneyland's Main Street while singing "Candy Man." The long pause was giving me hope and eventually an answer: "Let me get back to you on that, man," he groaned.

THE NEW ORIGINAL AMATEUR HOUR

This could be subtitled "TRAPPED IN HUMID ORLANDO FOR SIX WEEKS WITH WEATHERMAN WILLARD SCOTT AND OTHER FAT, SWEATY PEOPLE IN SHORTS." The show featured singers, tap dancers, novelty acts, and, for some reason, a lot of cloggers. Ted Mack had perfected this classic variety show in the '50s, and it had been a radio show in the '30s and '40s. I think they even had cloggers on the radio version. That must have been fun on the radio, just hearing the sound of clogs coming into your living room. Like the contestants, Willard was the perfect amateur. And like clockwork, he always annoyed me.

He would never say what was written for him in the opening monologue. You'd have to wait ten minutes until he was done with his hokey ad-lib chat to the audience. On his own, he never got a laugh, never even a chuckle. Every week, show after show, we all had to sweat out this routine until he finally would read the cue cards. He was one of those annoying performers who didn't think he needed a writer. There are a lot of those around. Names I won't mention. Tony Danza.

I couldn't stand Orlando. It was hot and humid, and I had to live in a hotel for six weeks. It was a plush but odd hotel, the Peabody. Every day at four o'clock, there was a parade of ducks marching through the lobby. I'm not kidding. Grown people would line up to take pictures of these mallards squawking through the hotel. This and Willard became too much for me, but I had to stick it out. This was pre-*American Idol* and, like its title, the talent was very amateur. You wouldn't root for any of these contestants to make it in show business. You just wanted them to make it to the door, not through the door. I learned patience, but it wasn't easy.

Out of over hundred contestants, one actually made it in show business: Aaron Carter. Ironically, he didn't win in his episode, some clogger did. Aaron became a teen star. Although, his career foundered in later years and he became bankrupt, I remember him as one of the bright lights in that series. I've tried to forget Willard. Ironically, he's still on *The Today Show*, having remarried at age eighty. I wonder if he and Aaron look each other up.

Classical violinist Jascha Heifetz once said, "A gig is a gig," but would *he* have written and produced a reboot of . . .

THIS IS YOUR LIFE

This was the classic '50s series in which host Ralph Edwards would surprise someone off the street and whisk them right away to the adjacent studio to remind them why they left home in the first place. Bogart, Bette Davis, James Cagney . . . He got them all. Years later, we got Angie Dickinson. There wasn't much of a story to her life, but she had done a couple of movies and TV shows, and NBC was glad we could get anybody. Of course, the big thing was the surprise. Nobody could ever tell the star about it. (For legal reasons, Angie's sister and agent signed off on it.) We told Angie's representatives that Brian De Palma wanted to interview her about the movie they did together, *Dressed To Kill.*

It looked like it was going to be a walk in the park. First of all, Angie loved that movie. It was her biggest film ever. But she wasn't that thrilled the day of the surprise. You could sense that she was in sort of "a mood." Like when the make-up girl approached her, she demurred, saying in a breathless voice, "No. I'm fine, I'd rather wait for Brian." But we barreled on. Pat Sajak, who was replacing Ralph Edwards as emcee, "bumped into" Angie with a script in make-up, telling her, "You've touched the hearts and minds of millions of people. You were everybody's *Police Woman*. You were everybody's girl next door. And tonight, Angie Dickinson, 'This Is Your Life.'"

And then I heard her sweet reply: "No fucking way," she exclaimed.

Now you have to understand that, next door, I had a huge studio audience watching this. I had Bob Hope in make-up, Burt Reynolds, half her family from North Dakota, and Angie in a very bad mood. She was starting to realize that there would be no Brian De Palma that night. Angie was not a happy camper, and neither was producer Ralph Edwards.

Nobody had ever walked off of *This Is Your Life*. Ever! Tonight was different. I could tell immediately there was no way she was going to do the show. But I walked in valiantly trying to change her mind. "Kenny? Are you involved with this?" she asked. "Yes," I said. "And it's gonna be fun and a frolic." I had never used that word in my life. She glared at me. "Fun and a frolic? Ha! Not for me," she declared. By then, a desperate Ralph Edwards had told her every single human being who was going to be on the show. So now, of course, there were not going to be any surprises, anyway—which was the whole idea of the show. The next thing I heard were the immortal words, "Angie has left the building."

Well, the audience was in shock. I did get a big laugh that day when I walked into the studio after they had seen the disaster. I said, "Bet you never saw that side of her, huh?" Needless to say, we had to come up with a new star within five days because we had airdates. So a week later we got . . . wait, I'll do it for you . . . I remember it exactly. It was so original. "You've touched the hearts and minds of millions of people. You were everybody's *Police Woman*. (I'm kidding. We dropped that line.) You were everybody's girl next door. And tonight, Kathie Lee Gifford, 'This Is Your Life.'" Don't ask. Speaking of no stories, the rest of the specials didn't go much better. Bea Arthur didn't want to appear on Betty White's *This is Your Life*. Ernest Borgnine didn't want to appear on Tim Conway's. Mrs. Conway insisted we buy Tim a racehorse. It died. Nobody wanted to appear on Barbara Mandrell's. Roy Scheider had no life. Dick Van Dyke was less-than-thrilled when Ralph announced to

America that Dick was an alcoholic. Some shows should just die off. Like the next one.

THE AMERICAN VIDEO AWARDS

This was about the lowest you could get, and that's why I'm mentioning it last in this chapter. But it paid big bucks. To sell this special, its producer had to invent an academy that didn't even exist: a new academy for video awards. It preceded the MTV awards, but, since nobody had ever heard of it, it was tough to book guests. It couldn't have been tackier. In fact, we bribed them just to show up. I even saw these so-called video stars grabbing envelopes of cash in the basement. It certainly wasn't prestigious for them, but they sure loved the greenbacks. It sort of was like graft from the old radio days. We did the best we could, spoofing awards shows to a degree, but I recall Tony Danza being rather lightweight and annoying as the host. He began the show off-script, not doing any of the jokes. A few of his ad libs got some giggles, so he started to stay off the script as written. When the laughter subsided and he tried to get back on the script, it was a little too late. He bombed the rest of the way. So did drummer Shelia E. We had given her a few lines after she opened the show but she refused to say them. Maybe she had a reason. I never did hear her talk, just bang.

NEIL DIAMOND . . . HELLO AGAIN

Dry ice . . . dry ice . . . dry ice.

BIGGER AND BETTER

I loved working on *Julie Andrews: One Step into Spring.* This special was a major perk because you got to work in London. A perk because you got to work with Julie, Leslie Uggams, and Leo Sayer. One drawback: the Muppets. They got paid more than me, and, while Kermit was sweet, Miss Piggy was a bitch.

Kenny with Julie Andrews

What really made this experience so memorable was the night I got to meet Prince Charles and Princess Diana. Rod Stewart's manager, Arnold Stiefel, had invited me to attend the Prince's Trust Gala at Wembley Stadium starring Rod, Paul McCartney, George Michael, Mick Jagger, and every other British superstar. At first I thought: No way. I'd rather go to the theatre. However, when I found out that Prince Charles and Princess Diana were going to be in attendance, I quickly changed my mind. If she was going to be in the "house," *I* was going to be in the "house." True, I was worried about the noise. But what the hell. I'd bring earplugs. I doubted I was going to meet her anyway.

But by night's end, not only had we met, but we both sort of fell in love with each other. Well, *I* fell in love with her. Who didn't? Let me explain the romance. After the show, it seemed their Royal Highnesses wanted to say hello and show their appreciation to all the stars who had just performed at the concert. And, luckily, all the stars' entourages were invited as well. The reception was held in this tacky Holiday Inn Ballroom across from the stadium, and attended by no more than thirty people. Not quite Buckingham Palace. No ice in the sodas. Stale tea sandwiches, the usual underwhelming British refreshments. My eyes fixated on the door. The British called it a "meet and greet." I called it "oy yoy yoy!"

You can guess whom I was looking for. Suddenly, just like in a movie, they appeared. The Royals were making their way to each star clump and giving their best wishes and greetings. Finally, there they were directly in front of me. Everyone in our clump was speechless except my friend Arnold, who incredulously bowed and called Diana, "Your Majesty." That's when I got my first laugh from her. I said to Arnold, "Not yet she's not, luv." She actually heard me and broke out laughing. I couldn't believe it. I got her attention and a laugh. A bit. I was on a roll. There was no way I was gonna stop. "How did you like the show?" I asked. Of course she said she loved it and I replied,

"Little too noisy for me." In an instant, she took out earplugs from her pocket saying, "It never fails." I knew now this was going to be a routine. I showed her my earplugs. She got hysterical.

Here's the unbelievable part of the story. As I'm taking in all this laughter, a gift from heaven, I hear a voice saying, "Kenny? Kenny Solms? What are you doing in London?" I looked over and I didn't even remotely recognize this woman, but no distraction was going to stop me from my hot streak. I turned to this stranger and said, "Right now I'm talking to the next Queen of England." The woman replied flatly, "You know the one thing about me. I never get impressed about people, no matter what they do." When Diana heard that, she literally screamed. She was in hysterics.

The prince, as they say, was not amused. Diana tried to defuse the moment, asking me if I had met her husband. Still on a roll and without missing a beat, I said, "Oh, please. Chuck and I went to high school together." To my amazement she broke up again. Even Charles laughed. I was in heaven. It was like that old song. "I danced with the man who danced with the girl who danced with the Prince of Wales." I was on a cloud. I had struck magic. Nothing could top it.

I just wanted to get out of there as fast as possible, savoring the moment. But just as life always has a habit of lurking around, so did I. I couldn't get out of the place. Nobody wanted to leave. Worse than that, no matter where I turned, I kept meeting Diana's eye and we both kept smiling. What a memory. What did I have left? There was a saving grace. From then on, every time I saw her face on a stamp, I could lick the back of her head.

Kenny with Joan Rivers

Joan Rivers and Friends: A Salute To Heidi Abromowitz was kind of an R-rated special. After all these years, it was fun to work with Joan again, but I had no idea what I was getting myself into. Shot in Vegas, this Joan Rivers romp had Joan roasting one of her favorite fictional characters: the slut, Heidi Abromowitz. It all took place in a ballroom. In fact, Joan's first joke was that Heidi was missing and, "would everyone look under their table?" As the evening wore on, the jokes got bluer. "She spent more time under men than barstools." "She uses Chapstick on her thighs." "A woman who's brought joy to millions of men without leaving her bed." "She was selling maps to her G-spot." "Her electric blanket has a control that says warm, hot, and next."

Among the filth, one of the sketches I contributed and liked was a *Lifestyles of the Rich and Famous* spoof. We had the actual host, Robin Leach, visit the site where Heidi once lived. He deadpanned, "Contented as a child and satisfied as a teenager, the home draws twenty thousand visitors per year. Most of them, boys and girls seeking their mother." There was nothing too dirty for Joan. For me it was a little too raunchy. But Joan got what she wanted from it: big ratings. As always, for Heidi it wasn't big enough.

Joan was another "bit" maniac. We never let phone conversations end normally. I always had to say something so she'd have to hang up on me. One particular memory was when I was in a pre-production meeting on her special and the production assistant said Joan was on the line. "Tell her I'll call her back." The production assistant said that Joan wanted me to know her husband Edgar had just killed himself and that Roddy McDowall was on his way over. Without missing a beat I said, "Tell her I'll call her back."

I miss Joan desperately. I had dinner with her just a week before her sudden death. We threw dinner rolls at each other. The shock of it all is still with me. She was such a force and the world seems just that much less without her spirit and energy. And now I have nobody who will hang up on me. The only slight consolation is that she had no idea she was going to die that day. Like all of us, she had thoughts about death. In fact, she once even told me she put in her will not to resuscitate her unless she could perform at least a ninety minute set onstage. She always wanted to give the audience their money's worth.

3 GIRLS 3

I really needed a kick in my career after all these specials. I got a lucky break when I sold a show to NBC called *3 Girls 3*. The critics loved it. It starred Mimi Kennedy, Debbie Allen, and Ellen Foley. The premise was onstage and offstage at a variety show, starring these three

Ellen Foley, Mimi Kennedy, and Debbie Allen

extraordinary and talented girls; Debbie, an incredible dancer, Ellen an inimitable singer, and Mimi, a fearless comedienne. Together, an incredible package. We had a wonderful staff of writers. One of them was Pat Proft who wrote two amazing sketches for Steve Martin, one of our guests. This was the first network show where Steve was paid top of the show. I was glad to pay it because I knew he'd be a big star. The first sketch had Steve showing off his new house to Mimi. It was revealed that the shrunken house only had a four-foot high-beamed ceiling, which forced Steve and Mimi to constantly bend and bob as they proudly walked around the house. When Mimi bumps into the beams, Steve boasts that he those put in. When he opens the drapes, we see a gardener but only from the waist down. A hilarious physical

sketch. The second Steve Martin sketch was set in a chic upscale inti-
mate café. When an upset Mimi complains to Steve, the fancy waiter,
that her husband was killed by the salad, he insists he must have heard
the order wrong. Mimi claims she ordered the Poisson dressing. A
nonchalant Steve said he thought she said, "poison" dressing. Mimi
claims her husband is allergic to poison. An unfazed Steve walks off
saying, "Well, there you are." Steve and Pat continued to collaborate
after that auspicious beginning.

It was the first time I really owned a show. I now had to think about
more than jokes: budgets, network meetings, tension. But I loved cre-
ating new stuff, breaking down the walls a little. Of course, NBC was
breaking me down a lot. This was the network that prided itself on a
real positive spin: "Least Offensive Programming." I swear. It's true.

John O'Connor in the *New York Times* wrote, "Instant stardom for
3 Girls 3. One of the most exciting and refreshing debuts that television
has offered in years." If only. It was cancelled after four shows.

By the time I sold another show to NBC, their executives had
changed. Thank God. It was now run by a young visionary, Brandon
Tartikoff. The show, *The Homemade Comedy Hour*, asked people to
send us their homemade videos—TV and movie takeoffs, imperson-
ations, even music videos . . . . Anything they thought was funny.
This was just at the beginning of the home video camera era where
people could film their own bits.

Brandon immediately ordered it as a special and was always a great
believer in the show. After it aired to not-great ratings but good reviews,
he even insisted we run it again. Then he made us a segment on Dick
Clark's *Practical Jokes and Bloopers*. He was determined. Unfortunately,
an ABC show was coming on at the same time, *America's Funniest
Home Videos*. That became a runaway hit. It was based more on bloopers and kids spitting up on each other. Really rank. Meanwhile, as I'm
writing this, they're still on the air and we're long gone.

I thought about suing, but this taught me another lesson. Try to get through life without ever suing anyone. Not only do you usually lose, but the only ones who make money are the lawyers. In this case, I doubt we would have stood a chance anyway. It turned out the ABC show was based on a Japanese television series whose premise was not exactly ours but close enough to withstand legality.

These almost-misses in television may drive you crazy, but they certainly drive you to another thing: Prilosec or other antacids.

By now I should have had an overall deal with NBC. I had been working steadily for them for years on all these specials and now came another one, *Kelsey Grammer Salutes Jack Benny*.

Like many of us, it seems Kelsey Grammer adored Jack Benny. Jack was his inspiration, and he wanted to salute him. We taped the show on the actual Jack Benny soundstage which coincidentally was CBS's Studio 33, where we taped the Burnett show. Needless to say, we used a lot of clips throughout the show. They were so much fun to look through and find the gems we needed for the special.

What I remember most was figuring out a way to put Jack and Kelsey on stage together actually doing a routine. Through the magic of computers and chroma key, Kelsey's dream came true. Side-by-side with Jack, and shot in black and white, it looked totally authentic.

Watching Kelsey with Jack, you can see that he has picked up a lot of Jack's mannerisms. The takes, the slowburns, the underplaying. These attributes obviously appeal to Kelsey and became part of his repertoire.

What I admired about Kelsey was the way he worked with writers. Whether it was from all those years on *Cheers* or *Frasier*, he really listened and never dictated. He was thoughtful, and he approached the show with an actor's focus. It was clear he idolized Jack Benny and wanted to show his genuine appreciation.

Carol gave me a chance to direct her in a television production of Neil Simon's *Plaza Suite*, three different stories all taking place in

Ad for Kelsey Grammer Special

the same suite at the Plaza Hotel. Directing was something I was always curious about, so I figured I'd give it a shot. While Carol played all three women, her three co-stars were the eminent Hal Holbrook, Dabney Coleman, and Richard Crenna. I was petrified. It was much too "in-your-face" for me. A director has to be constantly on his toes. I never knew what to expect from the actors. Their questions drove me crazy. Why am I doing this? Why am I walking over there? What does this mean?

The actors intimidated me, especially, when they couldn't take direction and kept arguing points of view. For instance, how do you tell a brilliant actor like Hal Holbrook that he was much too loud and much too serious and he should bring it all down? I soon gathered that the answer was innuendo. Carol got a kick out of seeing how I handled this delicate task. Dabney Coleman was a different kind of problem. He actually liked to argue and question all his motivations. One of those arguments was truly baffling.

In seducing the character of "Muriel," a girl he went to high school with, he was supposed to put his hand on Muriel's leg as he was talking about her beautiful brown eyes. It was a simple and obvious laugh, but only if he seductively grabbed her leg as he said "eyes." But he wouldn't do it, no matter how many times I mentioned it. "I'll find it, I'll find it," he kept reminding me. And he did. He saved it for the performance when there was an audience out front. Why he kept holding back, I'll never know, but I sure didn't like the contest. I found directing to be a battle of egos. As a writer you could stand on the sidelines and let the director do the dirty work. Let him pull out the performance.

My next problem with *Plaza Suite* was something I could do nothing about. During the live telecast, the show was interrupted by a news bulletin. Iraqi forces had just invaded Kuwait. Whatever audience we had was gone. And the network didn't help. When it came time to resume the show, instead of continuing where we left off, we were now in the midst of the next story, so nothing made sense.

My father pointed this out to me for years and wondered why ABC didn't run the show again instead of leaving viewers baffled. So Saddam not only killed millions of people, he ended my directing career. My father never forgave that monster.

While it's always fun being nominated for an Emmy, the novelty wears off when you're writing and producing the actual show. The 43rd Emmy Awards was a huge task. It's a three-hour telecast and it was Fox's first foray into the Emmy's. They were pulling out all the stops to make it an event. The big show needed three hosts: Dennis Miller, Jamie Lee Curtis, and Jerry Seinfeld. We cleverly gave the show a theme. With appropriate solemnity, a very serious James Earl Jones entered and declared, "Good evening. And welcome. Tonight, the Academy of Television Arts and Sciences invites you to join in a celebration of the American creative spirit as we pay homage to the many distinguished artists and gifted craftsmen whose consummate skill has raised primetime television entertainment to new heights of excellence." He ranted on, "Tonight, we salute these inspired visionaries and, with gratitude and humility, we dedicate the 1991 Emmy Awards telecast to—(A PIE FLIES INTO HIS FACE) comedy!"

It got a huge laugh and the comedy theme indeed carried the show along merrily. It took itself less seriously than usual. It fact it was even bawdy at times. When Kirstie Alley won her Emmy for "Cheers," she indeed acknowledged her statuette but said she was really looking forward to "the big one" giving a sly wink to her husband, Parker Stevenson, who was turning red in the audience. For some reason comedian Gilbert Gottfried couldn't resist making the show even bluer and segued into a monologue on masturbation. There were enough bleeps in that chunk to win a best song Emmy. The show ended up with the biggest rating heretofore for the Emmys so everyone was happy. Especially Kirstie.

BACK TO BROADWAY (OR SHOULD I HAVE STAYED HOME?)

In the mid-1980s, my good friend director Fritz Holt asked me if I'd be interested in writing a revue for Broadway. I said yes instantly because I was dying to get away from these TV specials. His idea was to celebrate the music and lyrics of Frank Loesser. I loved the idea. I idolized Loesser and I immediately came up with a title: *Loesser Is More*. Fritz liked it. Mrs. Loesser didn't. This begins my saga on "when the wife is still alive, she's gonna hate everything." Loesser's wife, the lovely Jo Sullivan, was actually a delight. Sweet. Funny. But very hands-on. While she was well aware that some of Frank's lyrics were very funny, she took him very seriously. This didn't fuse that well with my concept of the show, which I then called *Perfectly Frank*. I didn't want to write one of those "sit-around-the-piano-and-talk-about-the-guy" kind of shows.

The eras in Frank's short-lived life laid themselves out perfectly as departments . . . . The Army, Tin-Pan Alley, Hollywood Musicals, and Broadway Musicals. It gave me a chance to write sketches, spoofing all these eras and of course including his hit songs. Hollywood's USO, The Brill Building, The Piano Bar, The Soundstage, and Broadway Backstage. Jo was also in the show. This was an advantage and a disadvantage. While she sang brilliantly, the running gag featured her trying to talk about Frank, the man, the husband, the father, but I would never let her finish the sentence. Jo would say, "Few people knew that Frank liked to draw." Pam Myers would then interrupt her saying, "Few people care. Come along, dear," and drag her off the stage. Every time, Jo was interrupted. The audience loved the joke, but a few of her insiders were uncomfortable with the running gag.

I knew we were in a little trouble the night Mr. and Mrs. Danny Kaye came to see a preview in Los Angeles. Despite a sold-out and howling audience, the Kayes convinced Jo that the show was too irreverent, which was exactly what we all wanted. Everyone, that is, but the Kayes and now Mrs. Loesser. As in most pre-Broadway tryouts, suddenly all hell broke loose. The director was fired, cast members were replaced, and I was numb. Gail tried to cheer me up. Every time she came to rehearsals, she'd just turn to me and say, "Freeze it."

But chaos reigned. The new director, Ron Field, suddenly wanted all the sketches taken out of the show. He wanted to do a revered and refined Bell Telephone Hour type of show, rather an original and funny kind of stage revue. While he didn't dare cut the show-stopping "I Believe in You," a backstage sketch where everyone was falling in love with themselves in the dressing room mirror, everything else was fair game. He even colored Jo's hair, as if a new shade of red would suddenly make the show a hit.

I had no choice but to go to the Dramatists Guild, which isn't even a union. I was helpless. They were hapless. They gave me only one choice: If I wanted the show to continue, I could take my name off it. This was a show I conceived and spent a good part of a year writing, so it was a difficult choice. As usual, I summoned the troops from Philadelphia. I'd let it be their decision. I'll never forget my father's words at intermission: "It's not that bad. What's it gonna hurt you to keep your name on it?"

By the dreary curtain call, his mind had changed, signaled by a "thumbs down" gesture in my face. The only thing I remember my mother saying was, "Where's the car?" They had cleared the Holland

Tunnel before I was out of my seat. A year later, Fritz and I sold the original show to Showtime. It was without Jo and starred Cloris Leachman. It was a return to a happier time, but nothing erased that pre-Broadway pain. You hear these stories all the time about Broadway, but when you're in the story, it's not fun. Genius Larry Gelbart said it all: "If Hitler's still alive, I hope he's out of town with a musical."

The cast of *Perfectly Frank*

Why didn't I learn? I should have listened to Larry Gelbart. Well, who shouldn't listen to Larry Gelbart? And Woody Allen? And Neil Simon? And Nichols and May? And Mel Brooks? Not only are all of them geniuses, and all idols of mine, but all of them have been there and spoofed the out-of-town troubled musical. And yet, here I was again, with an out-of-town troubled musical. Whom was I listening to then? My agent. He thought this would be a smash. He was the only one. The place . . . San Diego. The show, *What The World Needs Now*, yet another musical revue, based on the songs of Burt Bacharach and Hal David, and directed by Gillian Lynne, the hugely successful choreographer of *Cats* and *The Phantom of the Opera*.

This time I used the songs to tell a love story. I wanted to take the conventional boy-meets-girl/boy-loses-girl/boy-and-girl-end-up-together dynamic: a mini-book musical, avoiding singing songs with no emotional through line. We had two wonderful leads, both unknowns who would soon become "knowns"—Sutton Foster and Patrick Wilson.

The first bad news came early. We lost Patrick Wilson in the middle of rehearsal. It isn't easy to find a replacement, and we had to just settle. Before we even left New York, our excitement level dropped. But we persevered. We were doing the show at the famous *Old Globe Theatre* in San Diego. Some of the not-too-bright actors thought it was England's original Old Globe Theatre. So did many of the locals, aiming their cameras to the building with reverence, as if Shakespeare had worked there. Although in her eighties, Gillian is a Broadway baby. She's used to big budgets, big sets, and big money. She could never address herself to the rules and regulations of being a LORT show.

LORT (League of Resident Theaters) is a contract for regional theatres, and Gillian could never deal with those realities. Once she saw the set, she didn't like it. Well, there was no money to change it. The same with the costumes. Neither of us realized until we were in

San Diego and running that there was no money even for rehearsals. Basically, we never had time to work on the show and make changes. Bacharach and David didn't help, either. Having seen the show only once and not collaborating with us in the beginning, their criticisms were too late to deal with as well. While they may sing, "What the World Needs Now Is Love," I knew what I needed: a plane ticket out of San Diego and *not* another musical revue.

Kenny with Burt Bacharach

UH-OH. ANOTHER MUSICAL REVUE.

I have always adored hit-maker lyricist Sammy Cahn. He was one of composer Jule Styne's best friends as well as a collaborator of his. They had won an Oscar for "Three Coins in the Fountain." I'd see him when Jule came into town. The late Sammy was a cheerful and funny guy who even wrote a parody of Jule's "Bye Bye Baby" for my fiftieth birthday.

MY BOY KENNY
REALLY STANDS OUT FROM THE MANY
HE IS RARER THAN RARE

MAY I SUGGEST, HE'S THE BEST
OF THE TALENTS I'VE MET
YOU CAN CHECK THIS WITH HIS DEAR FRIEND
CAROL BURNETT

AND I DAREN'T
EVEN MENTION DEAR MISS PARENT
AS YOU MAY BE AWARE

BUT KENNY'S ONE OF A KIND
WITH A MIND THAT'S SHOW-BIZ TOTALLY
SOMETIMES I THINK, HE THINKS, HE'S ME!!!
SOMETIMES I THINK, HE THINKS, HE'S ME!!!

I also knew Sammy's wife, Tita Cahn, from around town. So here I was again, developing a show with the wife of the late lyricist one more time. It was called, *Ain't That a Kick in the Head*. Chet Walker, a Fosse veteran, was choreographing and directing the workshop in New York. We had a terrific cast, and once again I was looking for an angle to keep the revue form fresh and new. Maybe one day I should just try to do the normal elements of a revue, first song, song, song, song, last song. This was a workshop, different from my two previous endeavors. For a limited amount of money, you do the show in a rehearsal hall without sets and costumes. You do two performances in one day. You invite producers and investors. This one was star-studded: Lauren Bacall, Hal Prince, Chita Rivera, etc.

I loved that they were there and they were supportive, but they had no intention of investing in a Broadway Show. While it went well, I'm still waiting for those checks. Otherwise, no show.

IT MUST BE HIM

A happy ending. Sort of. Finally, I got tired of writing *for* people, writing *about* other people, and writing *with* people. I wanted to write about my favorite person: me. Coming in a close second was Barbra Streisand. I decided to incorporate a lot of my actual life into a play. I wonder if you can guess what that must be about. Here's a hint. It's called *It Must Be Him.*

It Must Be Him tells the story of Louie Wexler, a whiz kid comedy writer from the heyday of variety television who is now out of luck and out of new ideas. With his devoted agent and considerably less devoted housekeeper by his side, Louie finds himself broke, lonely, and on the wrong side of middle age. Desperate to rekindle his fading career and save his Beverly Hills home, Louie searches high and low for one last shot at his own real-life happy ending. Sound like anyone you just read about? Want a copy for yourself? Just visit www.itmust-behim.com and order one.

The above summary was taken from the play's promotional packet. If only the project went as succinctly. Things never go as smoothly as that, making it very difficult to sell anything new. In television, I was lucky to get in when I was young. When you even hit your forties, in this day and age you're dismissed. With movies, your odds are even freakier. Of course you can get lucky, especially if you present a perfect package: a hot producer whose got a studio deal. Or if you attach one of the few saleable directors or a hot star.

I picked the theatre as it seems to be the only medium left that actually respects seniority, not to mention the residue of experiences you gain with age. In the theatre, that knowledge is actually respected; stories can be told, and you don't need the high-concept premises that dominate today's movies.

About twenty years ago, when *Les Miserables* was the hit of the decade, I had dinner with one of its directors, John Caird. He was a fan of *The Carol Burnett Show* and was anxious to know if I wanted to write for the theater. When I told him, "More than anything else in the world," he had one caveat: "Don't write your own life, whatever you do." I didn't quite understand what he meant by that, but I wasn't about to write about the French Revolution or the fall of Saigon. What did I know about that? I only knew my own life.

My theatrical experience up until now had been writing musicals about Lorelei Lee, Frank Loesser, Sammy Cahn, and Burt Bacharach. It may have taken a couple of decades, but I finally got around to writing about the one person I *really* know about: me. So, John, I hope you're not disappointed that I'm not storming the barricades of the Bastille or helicoptering out of Saigon.

Writing about one's life is probably what everybody should do when they hit sixty-five. It's freeing. It's a living diary. It perplexes. It stimulates. It rationalizes most of the things one never could justify in the first place.

Writing *It Must Be Him* made me come to terms with a lot of issues. My parents and the things I could never say to them when they were alive. My reflections. My feelings. My questions, the answered ones and the unanswered ones—and even theirs too. Essentially, *It Must Be Him* is about the struggle to grow up, to make peace with your parents and, most importantly, peace with yourself. In some weird way, it could be looked at as a tilted *Death of a Salesman*. Instead of a lot of drama, there's a lot of comedy. And it includes a movie! And a musical!!

Finally, *It Must Be Him* is a play about ageism, a subject I know well by living in Hollywood and working in the entertainment industry. After all these years, it's a universal problem. We live in a youth-oriented society, where you have to yell to be heard above the crowd. I hope I've done that with *It Must Be Him*. I also hope the audiences will be howling with laughter.

It might have taken a year or so to write the first draft. Then perhaps another six months to do revisions. Ironically, writing the play is easier than getting it produced. That's the tedious part.

The first way is to contact your agent . . . if you still have one. Since they can't read unless it's a two-page TV pilot pitch, that usually gets "Can you turn this into a feature?" or "You know Jack Nicholson. Send it to him." Bottom line, they couldn't care less about a play. In fact the only theatre they've probably ever seen is *Cats*, which they loved but didn't even understand.

A way to stir up interest in your play is to have a reading. You get friends to be the actors and someone you know to stage it, and you fill up the room with anyone you've ever known and, most importantly, anyone who laughs. There are all kinds of readings. There's the reading where people are just sitting in chairs reading the script. Then there's the staged reading where people move around a bit. Then you may go for the costumed reading. Sometimes the reading even has lighting, but that's about as extravagant as it gets. Never sets.

Of course, if you're a big star client at a big agency, you can send it to one of their theatrical agents in New York City. The snag here is that they think of you as a Hollywood writer and probably won't even read it unless you've attached Hugh Jackman, Denzel Washington, or at least one of the Kardashians. From there on, the process gets even more tedious. You send it to every theatre in the country: nonprofit, regional, foreign—basically any building that has a stage. You're lucky if you even get a form-letter rejection back from them. The bottom line to possibly get your play produced is money. The minute you mention it, these theatres are suddenly more interested, especially if the price is right. Your first natural instinct is, "*I* should pay for this? *I* should pay for something I've written free for the last two years?"

After a while and not much traction on the project, this cynical attitude subsides. I wondered, how much money would it cost to launch it in a small theatre? After another six months of hearing from nobody, you begin to ponder the money angle. Sure enough, the same people who rejected you a year ago are now returning your calls. Suddenly, they are complimentary about the play, and then if you know someone at the theatre and someone on their board likes it as well, maybe there's even a lunch. A dinner would mean real interest.

When you see that money indeed talks, naturally you go after the most prestigious theatre. I don't mean Broadway, where millions of dollars are involved, but a classy small theatre off Broadway would be ideal.

In my case, the classy Playwrights Horizons fit perfectly for *It Must Be Him*. It's a beautiful theatre on 42nd Street's Theatre Row, with about five hundred seats. It was going to be directed by Daniel Kutner, a protégé of Hal Prince's. He's a big talent with a great sense of humor. He got all my bits and sustained me with laughs during the entire experience. So did Larry Grossman and Ryan Cunningham, who wrote the musical chunk. And so did the cast who always got my bits in the play and off.

If your play does well in New York, it becomes a viable property. If it's a smash hit, you can even start thinking of moving it to Broadway. Of course, this would mean more money and more producers. But it's always a tempting decision. Who doesn't want their name in lights on Broadway? But how? The answer is obvious. It's all about money.

We had the cheap reading but invited affluent and successful producers. These are usually the fat cats or the yentas with blank checkbooks, the ones that favor musicals but you give it a shot. In our case, I had stellar actors (like Bob Balaban and Robert Klein) and prestigious producers filling the room. It couldn't have gone better. They were literally laughing in the aisles and our hopes were high. Too bad the money was low. Actually, none. What now? What was going to be the next step? In fact, was there a next step? Obviously, I needed someone with money to mount a production.

Putting in your own money is a dilemma. My brother was a successful real estate developer and he came up with a proposition. He'd put up half the money if I put up the other half. He had a reason. He was a very generous man, and it always rankled him that I was always on the more conservative side. In what he thought was a life-changing concept, he wanted me to finally put my money where my mouth was, so to speak. He claimed he always did it and it aggravated him that I wasn't as forthcoming in the cash department. I realized he was right. It wasn't a huge amount. Losing the money wouldn't change my life one way or another, so why not go for it? I looked on it as a maturation. Acting like a man. Taking responsiblity. Ironically, it really did feel good. I rationalized that it was like a plane ticket. Up to then, I always chose coach, though I could have afforded first. Although the money didn't come with any warm nuts, we were off and running once I signed that check.

We had a crackerjack staff. You always do in New York, as it's still where all the pros work and know what they're doing. The hierachy in mounting a play begins with the general manager. These are the people in charge of all the money. They make a meticulous budget indicating how much money you would need to make in order to break even each week and of course upwards or unfortunately downwards. All the expenses are detailed. The cost of the set, the lighting, the costumes, the sound, the publicity, the advertising, the theatre rental, the actors, the stage managers, etc. . . . Some of these fees even include royalties. Besides a small advance, this is where the writer and director make money. If you're a hit, which is amazingly rare in the theatre, you make a nice steady income. Smash hits can change a person's life. Cottage industry shows like *The Phantom of the Opera* and *Wicked* can make a writer a multi-millionaire. The average show usually makes you nothing. They even take your royalty out of any advance. Of course, when you're doing a show, you always pray that it's going to be a hit. You tend to avoid the reality that most projects are lucky to earn a penny. Most of them are losses, but, when you're in the middle of production, you're rather shortsighted. Everyone's usually very enthusiastic, dreaming of being the critics' darling and having a long run.

Auditions begin the process. I always find them interesting and exciting. With each audition comes another story. I do a funny thing at auditions that my directors seem to approve and get a kick out of. Before the actor reads or sings, I look at their resumes. I like to see if they're funny and smart improvisationally before they even read. There's always something funny to ask them. It loosens them up as well. The first thing I look at is their "Special Skills." "Oh, I see one of your skills is driving," I say. If they don't laugh, it's usually a hint that they're not funny. Some actors build on it with you because it makes them in on the joke because of my huge intensity in asking. When I ask them about their skills in archery, a whole improv is already in place. If I see a show they've done and it's a musical, I usually join them in a duet. It really relaxes the actor and makes the day go quicker, not to mention funnier.

When the reading begins, if they're all off right away I usually set them back on course. I can't stand seeing egg on their faces and letting them read too long if they're not getting it. Obviously, the director picks up on my comments and helps them along. It's a dicey process. You usually know the minute they enter the room if they're even remotely right for the part. If not, you hurry them along and try to be as sweet as possible. Needless to say, if you've already cast your lead, you hope that actor will come in and read with the other actors so the show becomes almost instantly alive. *It Must Be Him* cast Peter Scolari, Tom Hanks's buddy on *Bosom Buddies*. He was a delight to work with from the beginning. Peter's a natural and very smart. He has an inimitable style. He made the character his own from the beginning. Yet he externalized quite a lot of me the more I was in the room, and the more we rehearsed.

The character of Louie is so neurotic, but Peter made him likable as well. That's a thin line, and he never crossed it. He was perfect for the part, and he even drove stick shift. I never asked him about his prowess in archery.

As rehearsals grind on and on, your objectivity decreases. It's an intoxicating experience as the set reveals itself, the actors embellish their roles, you somehow make it through the first run-through, the first dress rehearsal, the first preview, and of course, you celebrate opening night with your friends, your family, celebrities, flashbulbs, flowers. It's all quite mesmerizing until the next morning. The reviews. One critic in the *New York Times* can determine life and death. Middling reviews usually mean middling results at the box office. The next day there's either a line at the box office, a trickle, or, at worst, nothing. It's not a good feeling to see no humans at the box office, except the staff inside who look pretty glum without much to do.

Sadly, this was the case for *It Must Be Him*. Most of the reviews were not positive. Of course, you cull them for quotes, but even that was an arduous task in our case. Then there's the agonizing question of how much money do we have for ads, anyway? Although the advetising budget is alotted, usually it's not enough if the reviews or positive word of mouth are not sufficient. You play mental games with yourself, thinking the audiences seem to like it and it's never empty, but usually you're just fooling yourself and blowing more money. Frankly, it's a hit-or-miss venture. Luckily, we were budgeted for a ten-week run, so it wasn't one of those one-night catastrophes. Too bad—I could have made money on the unused posters.

Our engagement went well. Audiences seemed to like it, and their positive reaction fulfilled me. Some nights. However, there are the rough ones too, when nobody's laughing and everybody's coughing. You even catch a few people dozing off. The secret nowadays is to try for one act so there's no intermission and no chance for walkouts. The few that do, you never seem to forget. They're usually the noisy couple schlepping coats and bags and asking each other who has the parking ticket. One occasion was unbelievably embarassing. An elderly couple, coats in hand, actually walked onto the stage itself during a performance and left through the door on the set, bewildering everyone in the audience, including the astonished actors who were on stage at the time. I'll also never forget a lady in the first row who got up as the show was ending and turned to her friend in the rear of the audience, giving her a thumbs-down gesture. That one. She couldn't keep her disdain to herself.

Once the show closed, I thought about my brother's investment advice. I'd like to say it put a smile on my face and that it made me feel more mature and wiser. The truth is I started flying coach again, hoping to eventually make up my financial loss on the play with a lot of cross-country flying.

Tragically, my brother, this kind and jolly giant of a person, died suddenly during the rehearsals. It was a huge blow to me. I was on such a high, and actually seeing an actor portray my brother on stage would constantly jolt me. The wound never heals. The irony is never lost on me that he never got to see the play he so believed in.

The New York company of *It Must Be Him.*

Your work on a project doesn't end when the show closes. Your next goal is to get the play produced somewhere else, and soon. Today, the Internet helps you connect to the thousands of theatres across the nation. We had to create a clever website to make theatre owners aware of the play and somehow communicate its comedic nature. After a website is created, you then send the play and the details of how to license it. I'm still waiting. I'm so tired of people bragging, "I got ten thousand hits today." I'm still waiting for one.

Obviously, my first choice for another production was Los Angeles. Besides being where I live, it's the second biggest market after New York. The Mark Taper Forum, the small boutique theatre of Los Angeles's Center Theatre Group, was my immediate first choice. Too bad they didn't think the same and unfortunately gave me an immediate no. While they liked it, they declined a production, as it had just played New York. Theatre Row, which is a clump of small theatres in a dingy part of Hollywood, didn't appeal to me. I don't think it appealed to them either since they rejected it too.

Then a coincidence happened. My father, who had died ten years earlier, had set up a charitable lead trust in his estate. The contribution had just ended, and I was awarded a nice sum of money with the provision that it could be used only for nonprofit organizations. Now, suddenly, the LA theatres were leaping at the chance to produce *It Must Be Him*. Once again, money talks. Now I had my choice of theatres. I picked Santa Monica's Edgemar Center for the Arts, a beautiful modern theatre in a posh area by the beach. The theatre attached one of its directors to the project and we were off and running, God knows to where.

I immediately saw that the dynamics for the LA production were not going to be as professional as New York. While New York demanded Actors Equity actors, Edgemar preferred non-equity actors. The reason obviously was money. They didn't want to pay actors much. In fact, hardly at all. As auditions began, I immediately saw the difference. In New York you had your pick of the finest actors in the city. Here, at a nonprofit theatre, you had to make do with what was available.

While everything about Edgemar was rank amateur, I got lucky and found a wonderful actor to play the lead: David Pevsner. Of course he was an Equity actor and gave the lead character of Louie a whole different spin. Peter was funny and playful in the New York production, but David gave Louie a gravitas that made the play more grounded and more dimensional.

Two sisters ran the theatre, and it could have been a Burnett sketch. Both were impossible. One sister was the diva who gave acting lessons to the poor suckers who signed up for her classes. The other was a ditzy blonde who knew nothing about the theatre. All she watched was the books to make sure that every department had minimal expense. Nonprofit? For whom, I wonder. Everything at Edgemar was shoddy. Even the tickets. They weren't real. They were stubs you get at a local carnival. Perfect for the circus this was becoming. There was one tiny and dirty dressing room for all the actors. The set was what you'd see in a high school. The budget for advertising was next to nothing. Closer to nothing. In fact, now that I remember it, it was nothing. They even made actors use the paint sink, which was only for brushes, not humans. Costumes—forget about it; there were none. She told people to wear their own clothes. I'll never forget the missing prop story. When we came back Tuesday after a dark Monday, the set was missing its desk and a few lamps. The stage manager was panicking. She soon discovered the problem. It seems the blonde producer had taken a fancy to them and moved them to her office. Can you imagine? She didn't know what the big deal was.

Ironically, on stage the show gelled and really worked. Audiences were touched by it, and laughs were aplenty. This time, the critics were kind. I should have had a smile on my face, but, because of the poor management, there was always a problem. The producer wouldn't pay for the actors' parking. Something on the ramshackle set was always breaking down . . . . And so was I.

Opening night almost took me over the edge. Unfortunately, the dimwitted producer had invited too many critics and there were more people than there were seats. What's worse was that she wasn't even around. She picked opening night to take her kid to the circus. As frantic as I was, bits pulled me through this one. I explained the situation to the audience, and they were roaring with laughter at my frustration. Joan Rivers, Michelle Pfeiffer, Lily Tomlin, Carol Burnett, and Tim Conway were all roaring from my nervous breakdown. While the producer was out somewhere watching a high-wire act, I had to beg my friends to sit on the steps. Now I was worried. Were my bits getting too many laughs? Would the play suffer from it? Against all odds, the performance was stunning that night and played without a hitch. Of course, I never asked the people on the steps what they thought about it. I don't even know if they survived. They might have been trampled to death.

AS THE STOMACH TURNS

Over the years, I've been successful pitching screenplay ideas to studios and even getting deals to write scripts. It isn't easy. Doing it is like a performance. A lot of bits and then you sneak in with the pitch. If you're incredibly lucky, you land the deal, but calm down. It doesn't mean they're going to film it. Michael Black, a Hollywood agent and friend of mine has the perfect phrase for it . . . "Don't get dressed," he warns. I have some of those scripts lying on my desk right now. At least with them, you can console yourself that you were paid. However, the pitching process has slowed down in this town. Then you wonder why people say they're pitching again. Another breath.

Your agent is always hollering, "Write a spec script, write a spec script." "Spec" means speculative. You write it on your own, but you own it totally. It's always easy for an agent to suggest, but do they ever have an idea for one? Coming up with an idea isn't easy. I must have another ten of those sitting on my desk right now. They're a tough breed to sell. You need to attach a producer, a writer, or a star—and, of course, you need the idea.

What to do? What to do? Then I had an inspiration. Maybe I should go back to where it all began. Years ago on the Burnett Show we did a hilarious sketch called "As the Stomach Turns." Why not bring it back? Thirty-five years later, Carol could still be sitting in that same chair in Canoga Falls waiting for the next scandal to arise.

Carol and Lucy in the original *As The Stomach Turns*

What would it be? Who's coming up from the basement? Who's coming down from the attic?

I got so excited that I immediately called Carol and pitched it to her. She agreed with me that it was a natural. Bring Marian back. Put her in some jeopardy. Invent new characters with new traumas. Call it, "As the Stomach *Still* Turns."

Carol did caution me that I'd have to write it on spec in order for the network to even understand the premise. However, it was clear that she was excited, so I proceeded. I assumed Carol would be a great name to be attached to a new half-hour show, and hilarious ideas were bursting out of me left and right. New jeopardies, new characters, but with Carol at the helm.

Six weeks later, I gave the script to Carol. I was thrilled when she called to tell me it was hilarious. I was less thrilled when she made it perfectly clear that she wasn't walking into any network executive's office in person to pitch herself for the show. That was a little discouraging, but I had no choice but to move on. I'd keep the idea going, still attaching Carol to the deal.

I called Carol's agent in hopes of encouraging him and the agency to form a package so we could pitch it together. He soon got back to me and said that while Carol was indeed interested, she'd only appear in the pilot.

What? Excuse me? What good would that do? Why would a network buy a series without the leading lady being attached to all the episodes? The truth was that Carol was in no mood to do a regular series anymore. She confided to me that it would just be too much work, but as a friend she would help me out by doing the pilot. That wouldn't do. I knew she meant well, but without Carol there's no show. There's no Marian.

But there is for you. As a little treat, I have added the pilot script to the end of the book for your enjoyment If you like it, write Carol. Maybe you'll change her mind. Better yet, write to the networks. You are their audience. Don't they owe you something?

CURTAIN CALL

As a kid, I used to fantasize about curtain calls and in fact I would actually do them in the privacy of the basement of my home. Nobody could see me there, and I could imagine anything I wanted. Bowing was the essential "bit." I pretended I was all the performers in the show. If it was a play, the bows would all be very intense and not very grandly staged. They were just a sort of intense and weary look, as if the actors were showing the audience how rough it's been for them to share their burdened duties to the play and a thank you for all their hard work. In comedies, they were a little more theatrical, using the set as entrance and exit points for the bows. All very up and energetic, down a staircase, behind a plant. Cute. For a musical, I'd start with the quick bow for the chorus, the build to the supporting players, and finally the most exciting of all . . . the last bow for the star.

I've always been curious if the last bow is in the star's contract. Are they thrilled? Are they embarrassed at all that attention? I used to talk about this to Carol, who hated curtain calls. She always thought they were indulgent and embarrassing: a "look at me!" in the spotlight, intimidating her. They made her feel awkward, too much of a "love me, love me" ego trip. Others obviously adore them and relish their theatricality. Liza Minnelli's are bigger and bolder, staged with particular precision and flair. Angela Lansbury's curtain call in *Mame* was a thing to behold. As I recall, she made her entrance downstage and then embraced everyone in the cast with great warmth before turning and bowing to her wildly appreciative and of course, standing audience.

This whole fascination with bows started in my early teens after being exposed to them in the pre-Broadway tryouts that were constantly playing Philadelphia. They were my first exploration into fantasy, being recognized, being adored. Growing up as a kid, I used to spend hours working on those bows, closing my eyes and feeling the love and imagining thunderous applause. I dragged them out, perfecting and polishing them, always frightened that someone would open the door and discover me, catching me in the act.

Those fantasies were the first "bits" in my life. As I grew older they took on a new dimension. When I decided to become a writer and not a performer, the bowing thing subsided. Thank God! All that bowing was starting to weaken my knees. However, the need to make people laugh and get attention just increased. It's a good thing I made my career in show business where you aren't the only one carrying on like this.

Comedy writers and performers are no strangers to this myth of merrymaking. Obviously, the need must come from a lack of something deeper. Without getting into the psychology of it, one can see it as odd behavior, an eccentricity. Everyone has a personality, and, if it's not harming yourself or others, this isn't the book to analyze such behavior. All the dogma about the so-called funny people hiding something darker is no doubt an interesting premise, but not the one to be dwelled on in this book. I doubt that I could anyway, as I don't claim to be a doctor, a psychologist, or a scientist. In fact in high school, I burnt the Bunsen burner in science class having no idea what it was or what it was supposed to be. I still don't get it, although I do remember making coffee in it once, just to get a laugh.

In my mother's yearbook, they quoted her as saying she would talk to a stone. I obviously picked up that trait. I've always been talking and doing bits to get through the day, to get through life, and to get through this book.

Excuse me. The doorbell just rang. I've got "bits" to do.

BONUS MATERIAL

AS THE STOMACH STILL TURNS

AS THE STOMACH
STILL TURNS

The script for the unproduced television pilot
by Kenny Solms

SCENE ONE

INT. MARIAN MORGAN LIVING ROOM — DAY

The setting is the infamous Marian Morgan
living room, a living room often visited on
the "The Carol Burnett Show." Since it's been
over thirty years, the living room is dusty
and even has cobwebs. Peering through them is
MARIAN, played once again by Carol Burnett.
Even though it's years later, she's still
sitting at the same small dining table by the
window, having some coffee. A tiny suitcase
is standing by the front door.

> ANNOUNCER (V.O.)
> When we last left Marian, over
> thirty-five years ago, the lovely
> lady of Canoga Falls was a vital,
> beautiful woman.

Marian smiles and pats some dust and cobwebs
off her hair.

ANNOUNCER (V.O.)
But the years have not been kind.

Marian shoots a look.

ANNOUNCER (V.O.)
They've taken their ghastly toll.

Marian shoots another look.

ANNOUNCER (V.O.)
Not only have her looks faded, but
her memory is only a memory, and
her . . .

MARIAN
(not able to hold back)
Oh, shut up!

ANNOUNCER (V.O.)
Marian, have I said something to
offend you?

MARIAN
No. But this coffee is freezing.
Oh. And I'm going to have to let
you go.

ANNOUNCER (V.O.)
Why? Why? Why?

MARIAN
One question at a time. It's
because I'm broke, broke, broke. I
have to leave my treasured home.

ANNOUNCER (V.O.)
Marian, I hate to break it to you,
but this place is not that great.

MARIAN
I have no choice. It's either that
or . . .

ANNOUNCER (V.O.)
Suicide?

MARIAN
I'd shoot you before I shot myself.
There's no denying it. If I want to
keep the house, I'll have to find a
renter. Someone clean. Someone who
can take care of my things. Someone
who will . . .

ANNOUNCER (V.O.)
Keep me on.

MARIAN
That will be up to Fair Warnings.

ANNOUNCER (V.O.)
Fair Warnings?

MARIAN
The retirement home.

ANNOUNCER (V.O.)
Poor Marian. Will she ever find a
renter?

SOUND: Doorbell.

MARIAN
That was fast. Who knows? Maybe
somebody has come to my rescue and
I can just stay here. Maybe it's
even Mister Right.

Marian answers the door. A hunky male PUNK
ROCKER stands there clad in black leather and
long hair with a motorcycle helmet in his
hand.

>   MARIAN (cont'd)
>   Wrong!

>   PUNK ROCKER
>   I'm looking for a room.

>   MARIAN
>   One where you'll blast music in,
>   burn down, and do heavy drugs in?

>   PUNK ROCKER
>   If we have time. We only need it
>   for an hour or so.

>   MARIAN
>   We?

A SKANKY-LOOKING GIRL enters the doorway.

>   SKANKY-LOOKING GIRL
>   Hi.

>   MARIAN
>   Why don't you two healthy, all-
>   American kids try the Canoga Falls
>   Y? Both "M" and "W."

>   PUNK ROCKER
>   We did. They told us to come here.
>   They said you were the only woman
>   crazy enough . . .

Marian closes the door in their faces. She
goes over to the sofa and throws pillows into
her suitcase.

MARIAN
"Save for a rainy day." Ha! "The
meek shall inherit the Earth."
Please!
"For a Good Time Call Marian." I'm
still waiting for that call.

MARIAN (cont'd)
(sighing)
How can I ever leave my Canoga
Farms's farm? True, I never grew
anything on it. I never had chick-
ens or goats or cows. But I had
love. I had friends.

SOUND: Doorbell

MARIAN (cont'd)
I'll get it.

Marian adjusts to the mistaken sound cue and
opens the door. In the doorway stands DEBRA
MAXWELL, an attractive woman in her mid-40s
(LISA KUDROW).

DEBRA
Hello, I'm Debra Maxwell, an attractive woman in my mid-thirties.
(Marian stares at her.)
Forties. You could call me the new
kid on the block.
(Marian stares again)
Okay. New woman on the block. I've
just come to Canoga Falls after a
bad marriage, a failing career, a
jail term, and a bad mani/pedi, but
with a new lease on life.

                    MARIAN
          (guiding her into the living room)
     And hopefully one in your handbag.

                    DEBRA
     How did you know?

                    MARIAN
     It's a small town. News travels
     fast. And as luck would have it,
     I'm also a notary.

                    DEBRA
     Oh, good.

                    MARIAN
     That'll cost you ten dollars.

                    DEBRA
     Oh, this house is everything I've
     ever hoped for.

                    MARIAN
     That's good.

                    DEBRA
     Except for the outside and all the
     furnishings. But I like the price.
     Sit down, Marian.

     Of course, Marian has been seated. Debra is
     still standing.

                    DEBRA (cont'd)
     My story is much too sad to be told.

                    MARIAN
     Excuse me, Debra are you going to
     sing?

　　　　DEBRA
No, but I could use a little organ
music.

Marian nods to cue organ music. Debra tries
to tell her story but has to compete with the
crescendo-ing music.

　　　　DEBRA (cont'd)
I come from a very small town. My
family were good people. Plain
people. Poor people. Ugly people. I
always wanted to be better than
them . . . which was pretty easy. I
worked my way through college.

The music is becoming too loud, and Marian
finally has to hurl a dish to silence the
organist, who reels in pain.

　　　　DEBRA (cont'd)
It was my goal to become a thera-
pist. I'll never forget that look
on my parents' faces at my gradua-
tion.

　　　　MARIAN
They must have been touched.

　　　　DEBRA
They were humiliated. I caught them
selling my diploma.

　　　　MARIAN
Is this story going anywhere, dear?

　　　　DEBRA
Why? Do you think it could be a
musical? Besides being a wink-wink
psychiatrist, I'm a composer, a

lyricist, but most importantly,
somebody you can trust. Somebody
you will love having in your home.
Guarding it. Loving it. Protecting
it. An upright citizen whose values
are the highest. Wholesome. Trust-
worthy. Honorable.

> MARIAN
And so funny. A laugh a minute.

> DEBRA
Oh, I'm sorry. Have I been going on
for too long?

> MARIAN
Yes, and the folks from Fair Warnings Villas are about to pick me
up. As you can see, I'm already
packed.

She indicates the one tiny suitcase that's
still sitting by the door.

> DEBRA
Are all your life's possessions in
there?

> MARIAN
It's been a rocky road.

> DEBRA
Well, you can always count on me.
Here's one month's rent and one
month's deposit.
>   (hands Marian a check)
I'll never ever be late. Come the
first of the month, you'll always
have my check.

                    MARIAN
That's wonderful. Just wonderful
news.

                    DEBRA
You remind me of someone.

                    MARIAN
Really?

                    DEBRA
Yes, like an annoying old friend.

SOUND: Doorbell

                    MARIAN
                    (flatly)
I'll get the door.

As Debra checks out the living room, Marian
opens the door to reveal NAN, Marian's next-
door neighbor. She's middle-aged and chatty.

                    NAN
Hello Marian.

                    MARIAN
Nan!

                    NAN
I'm Jan.

                    MARIAN
Oh Nan, you poor darling.
                    (to Debra)
She has amnesia.

                    NAN
I do?

MARIAN
See? She already forgot.
(to Nan)
This is Debra Maxwell. She's thinking of renting the house.

NAN
Oh no. Not that again.

MARIAN
Nan, face it. I have no choice. All
my savings are gone. Nothing is left.

NAN
I'll lend you money.

MARIAN
I need thousands.

Beat.

NAN
(reconsidering and crossing to
Debra and embracing her)
Debra, tell me all about yourself.

DEBRA
I come from a small town. My family
were good people. Plain people . . .

MARIAN
(interrupting)
None of that is important now.
Debra, you were about to sign the
lease, and old Nan here was about
to rest.
(opening door for her)
Bye, Nan. Don't forget to take your
medication.

                    NAN
    What am I on?

                    MARIAN
    Everything. As always.

                    NAN
    Oh. I forgot.
            (to Debra)
    Nice meeting you.
            (to Marian)
    Call me when you know your plans.

                    MARIAN
    I will. Collect.

    Nan exits. Marian closes door.

                    DEBRA
    She seems sweet.

                    MARIAN
    She's not. She's a nightmare like
    everyone else in this town.

    Marian sits down.

                    DEBRA
    Sit down, Marian.

                    MARIAN
    More story?

                    DEBRA
    I'm afraid so. You see I used to
    live in the big city. Going here,
    going there, meeting him, meeting
    her, talking, walking . . .

MARIAN
You were busy.

DEBRA
But I was stalked.

MUSIC: Organ sting

MARIAN
(looks to the side)
I haven't heard that in quite
awhile.

ANNOUNCER (V.O.)
It's one of my favorite tunes.

MARIAN
(to Debra)
Go on, dear.

DEBRA
It was awful. He followed me wher-
ever I went.

MARIAN
Like a constant shadow?

DEBRA
I never thought of it that way.
What an interesting description!

MARIAN
Which reminds me. Is there much
more to the story?

DEBRA
I hope not. I just want to be away
from it all. I want to be safe.

MARIAN
(turns on alarm)
I have the best alarm system in
Canoga Falls. You'll never have to
worry about anything here. Relax.
You came to the right place. And
you rented the right home.

DEBRA
(reminding Marian)
At the right price!

MARIAN
Don't push it, Debra.

DEBRA
I just want a simple life in a
simple town with simple people like
yourself.

SOUND: Car honk

MARIAN
(picking up suitcase)
There's my simple ride. Maybe I'll
come visit you sometime.

DEBRA
Wonderful. How about a year or so?

Marian opens the door and takes one last look
at the living room and sighs.

MARIAN
I don't know how I'll ever get over
this house.

DEBRA
Try.

Debra closes the door on Marian.

                    DEBRA (cont'd)
          I need a drink.

Marian pushes the door back open.

                    MARIAN
          Too bad. It's all in my luggage.

Debra slams door. Debra turns around and sees
her STALKER entering from the kitchen. He's a
tall man in his 40s, looking sinister in a
trench coat.

                    STALKER
          You think you could really get away
          from me?

                    DEBRA
          Stalker! What are you doing here?

                    STALKER
          Still stalking you. We'll be so
          happy here.

                    DEBRA
          Over my dead body.

                    STALKER
               (walking towards her)
          Yeah. That's usually the way it
          ends up.

Marian rushes back into the house.

                    MARIAN
          Debra, I forgot my purse and . . .

She stops when she sees the Stalker.

MARIAN (cont'd)
(cutesy)
Naughty Debra. You didn't tell me
you had a roommate.

DEBRA
Marian, this is the stalker I was
telling you about.
(introducing)
Marian. Stalker.

STALKER
Hello.

MARIAN
Debra was telling me all about you.

STALKER
I'll bet.

MARIAN
You should really leave her alone.

STALKER
You should really get a new alarm
system.

MARIAN
(to Stalker)
Get out!

DEBRA
Marian, I can take care of this
myself.
(to Stalker)
Get out!

STALKER
Why don't you try to make me?

                    MARIAN
          Can I?

Marian calmly walks to the fireplace, grabs
an anvil, and hits him over the head. He
falls to the floor.

                    DEBRA
          Marian! You didn't even know him.

                    MARIAN
          But you did and you didn't like
          him. You're my tenant. I have to
          take care of you.

                    DEBRA
                    (sweetly)
          Ahh!

                    STALKER
                    (grimacing in pain)
          Ahh!

                    MARIAN
          You again?

Marian hits him again.

                    MARIAN (cont'd)
          C'mon, we gotta get rid of the
          body.

                    DEBRA
                    (frightened)
          Then I'm an accomplice.

                    MARIAN
          Well, I can't pick him up alone.

Marian begins to wrap body in rug.

                    DEBRA
How do you even know he's dead?

                    MARIAN
                    (looking in rug)
He looks pretty shabby to me. Come
on, let's haul him out of here.

                    DEBRA
                    (helping her)
One question, Marian.

                    MARIAN
What is it?

                    DEBRA
Do you intend to replace the rug?

Marian shoots her a look.

                    <u>END OF SCENE ONE</u>

SCENE TWO

EXT. FAIR WARNINGS VILLAS - DAY

It's a brick and brass affair with the
lantern lighting and the pretty lawn, but God
only knows what's inside.

INT. FAIR WARNINGS VILLAS - DAY

While a constant flow of NURSES, PATIENTS,
and AIDES are busily passing by, Marian,
with her tiny suitcase, is at the front desk.
SEBASTIAN, a gay male nurse in his thirties,
is behind the desk, obviously giving Marian a
hard time while he enters her information on
his desktop computer.

> SEBASTIAN
> (sassy)
> Honey, I don't like these Q and A's
> any more than you do, but we have
> regulations and you're gonna have
> to deal with it and me. God knows,
> I know it isn't easy.
> (flatly)
> And what's with the bloody hand?
> Don't tell me. You just killed
> somebody.

He laughs at his own joke. Paranoid, Marian
hides her hand.

> MARIAN
> You are so funny.

SEBASTIAN
I know. Know anyone cute? Likes
musicals? Physically fit? Was at
Barbra's last concert?

MARIAN
Could we just get on with this?

SEBASTIAN
(under his breath)
Hmm, another bitch. What was the
name of your first dog?

MARIAN
You're not serious.

SEBASTIAN
Honey, I'm just . . .

MARIAN
Alright, alright. Queenie.

SEBASTIAN
How dare you!

MARIAN
What? That was the name of the dog.

SEBASTIAN
First car?

MARIAN
Are these questions really necessary?

SEBASTIAN
If you want to get in here. You
know like the brochure says. Three
meals a day. Bingo, two nights a
week. Every Sunday, some lousy
movie edited for seniors.

MARIAN
Alright. I never had a car. I
always took the bus.

A buzzer from the computer goes off.

SEBASTIAN
Ooh, not a good answer. We'd better
just scroll down to your finan-
cials.

MARIAN
It's not very good.

SEBASTIAN
I can see. What are you doing here,
anyway? You'd have a better shot at
assisted living. You don't have a
chance in hell of getting in here.

MARIAN
But my doctor said . . .

SEBASTIAN
I don't care what your doctor said.
You don't got the bucks for Fair
Warnings.

MARIAN
My doctor said I was a special
case.

SEBASTIAN
Aren't we all?

MARIAN
(desperately)
Alright. I slept with my doctor.

                    SEBASTIAN
I wish I could say the same, but
his wife and children are always
hanging around.

                    MARIAN
Please!

                    SEBASTIAN
                (looking at computer)
Oh, I see it now. Compliments of
Dr. Klein. Don't worry, honey. Your
secret's safe with me.
                (as if in a department store)
Slut in the house!

Marian is mortified.

                    END OF SCENE TWO

SCENE THREE

INT. MARIAN'S ROOM - FAIR WARNINGS - DAY

It's cozy and pink. The only problem is
that there are two single beds with GERT
ROSENBLATT, a hefty woman in her mid-to-late
70s, sitting on one of them. As Marian
enters, she is quite surprised.

              MARIAN
     Sorry, there must be some mistake.
     I was promised my own room.

              GERT
     Don't tell me. You slept with Klein
     too?

              MARIAN
     Yeah. He convinced me I had to
     move.

              GERT
     Yeah I know the whole bit. That you
     couldn't take care of yourself
     alone?

              MARIAN
     And that I couldn't afford it.
          (realizing)
     It's my fault. What was he doing
     looking into my bank account any-
     way?

              GERT
     What was he doing looking into your
     underwear?

MARIAN
The same thing.

GERT
He was faking you out!

MARIAN
He wasn't the only one faking. That
sex maniac! He's the reason I'm
renting out my house.

GERT
I lost my condo. We bought his
romancey crap and now we're both
homeless.

MARIAN
It's a harem!

GERT
Damn straight! You should see the
B ward. They can't walk straight
anymore. The man is an animal. I
can't believe he still practices
medicine.

MARIAN
Thanks a lot, Obamacare. We gotta
get out of here.

GERT
I've been trying for two weeks.

MARIAN
Oh please. We'll climb out a window.

GERT
They're electrified.

MARIAN
How about the exits?

GERT
Sealed.

MARIAN
The fire escapes?

GERT
Oh, they left here a long time ago.

MARIAN
How's the food?

GERT
Not bad. The movie, though, was
horrible. It was that "Les Mis-
érables." It was like they were
singing on your face. Oy.

MARIAN
Gert! Get a grip! We need to get
out of here and find a place to
live.

GERT
Well, I do have a cousin in Cleveland. Maybe she'd take us in.

MARIAN
Great! But how the hell do we get
out?

END OF SCENE THREE

SCENE FOUR

INT. MARIAN MORGAN LIVING ROOM - DAY

Debra and her new neighbor, Nan, are having
coffee. The only change in the room is a
bright new rug.

                    NAN
          Well, dear. I must say things look
          pretty much the same around here.
                    (beat)
          But what's with the new rug?

                    DEBRA
          Oh, Marian gave it to me.

                    NAN
          She's so generous.

                    DEBRA
          She is?

                    NAN
          To a fault.

                    DEBRA
                    (blurting it all out)
          Exactly. It was all her fault. I
          had nothing to do with it.

                    NAN
          What? What are you going on about?
          Calm down.

DEBRA
(to an already seated Nan)
Sit down Nan. I need to talk you
about Marian. Something terrible
happened here the very day I moved
in.

NAN
Wait a minute. I think I know where
you're going with this.

DEBRA
You do?

NAN
Debra, did you throw up on Marian's
pretty oriental rug?

DEBRA
What? That's disgusting. Nan, can I
trust you?

NAN
Of course you can. What's a next-
door neighbor for anyway? You can
always count on me. You can always
tell me anything.

DEBRA
(nervously)
Well . . .

NAN
That's it?

DEBRA
It's a little more involved.

NAN
I have all the time in the world.

                    DEBRA
When I was living in the city ...

                    NAN
Oops, gotta go.

Nan gets up. Debra pushes her down and con-
tinues her story.

                    DEBRA
I discovered that much to my dismay
I had a stalker.

                    NAN
Was he cute? Tell me everything.

                    DEBRA
Nan, this is serious.

                    NAN
So am I. Canoga Falls is pretty
quiet.

                    DEBRA
I feared for my life. It became so
serious I had to hire a detective.

                    NAN
Was he cute?

                    DEBRA
Nan!

                    NAN
I'm sorry. Ever since I've stopped
watching soap operas, my life's
been so dull.

DEBRA
(continuing story)
Just when I thought I had a hold on
him ...

NAN
Mmm ...

DEBRA
Just when I thought I had a grasp
on him ...

NAN
(more excitedly)
Mmmm...Do you think he could find
his way to these parts?

DEBRA
Not the parts you're talking about.
Besides, he was here!

NAN
Sting!

DEBRA
He was in this house!

NAN
Louder sting!

DEBRA
Nan, do you want to hear this story
or not?

NAN
Are you kidding? I want to meet
him.

DEBRA
He's dead.

                    NAN
          (disappointed and getting up)
Oh. You have any other stories?
Otherwise, I have to go. I have
stuff in the dryer.

                    DEBRA
Marian is the one who killed him.

                    NAN
Oh, that Marian. She's always
spoiling everyone's fun.

                    DEBRA
Oh, Nan, what am I going to do?

                    NAN
It's always about you, isn't it?

                    END OF SCENE FOUR

SCENE FIVE

DISSOLVE TO:

EXT. FAIR WARNINGS VILLAS - DAY

Marian and Gert, both now disguised as nurses in white uniforms, sneak along the glass, trying to be invisible. They each have their luggage. Gert even has a shopping bag.

> MARIAN
> Hurry up, Gert. We're almost out of here.

> GERT
> I hate this outfit. It put pounds on me.

> MARIAN
> Funny, how that happens. Just think, honey, if we get out of here, you'll have a lifetime to lose them.

Sebastian runs after them carrying a large net.

> SEBASTIAN
> Come back here you bitches! Klein's gonna have my ass!

> GERT
> Please! He's had mine for five and a half months!

END OF SCENE FIVE

SCENE SIX

INT. MARIAN MORGAN'S LIVING ROOM - DAY

Debra and Nan are still sitting at the table,
still having coffee.

     DEBRA
I don't know if I can take it anymore.

     NAN
The coffee?

     DEBRA
No, the murder! I could never live
with it.

     NAN
Let Marian take the rap. She's the
one who killed him. Besides, she
deserves it anyway and she knows
why.

Marian storms into the house.

     MARIAN
I do?

     NAN
      (covering herself)
Look Debra. It's our darling,
darling Marian!

     MARIAN
Oh, knock it off, Nan. I heard
everything. And so did my newfound

best friend, Fat Gert.
Gert walks in chomping on a chicken
drumstick and closes the door.

                GERT
Anybody got salt? This is so dry.

                MARIAN
This whole money thing was a hoax.
He was just conning me. Dr. Klein
just wanted our bodies. Twenty-four
hours a day at his own whim.

                NAN
That doesn't sound so bad. I've
been available since the Clinton
administration and Klein never put
his hands on me.

                MARIAN
It's my fault. I always used to
think his bark was bigger than his
bite.

                GERT
Who would've thought his bite would
satisfy most of the women in Canoga
Falls?

                NAN
My luck I stopped seeing him. Dr.
Chow brings nothing to the party.

                DEBRA
Marian, I didn't tell her anything.

                MARIAN
Oh, please.

DEBRA
Well, just the shooting part.

MARIAN
If you two think you can pin this
rap on me, I have news for you.

NAN
What are you talking about?

DEBRA
News? What kind of news?

MARIAN
This kind of news.

She turns on the television and it's
instantly "This Kind of News" News Show.

TV ANCHOR (ON TV)
Welcome to "This Kind of News."
Today an unidentified carpet was
found floating in the Canoga Falls
Falls. The ugly bloodstained oriental rug could only have belonged to
Marian Morgan or her new tenant,
Debra Maxwell, or even her next
door neighbor, Nan Benedict, who
was last seen in the Morgan back-
yard with pool boy Manuel Vargas.
Vargas has been ruled out as a
suspect.

NAN
Turn it off. The only thing I ever
gave Manuel was a piñata.

Marian turns off the television.

                    DEBRA
Well they didn't find the body.

                    MARIAN
Not yet. Face it, girls. We're all
in this together.

                    GERT
I don't even know any of you.

                    MARIAN
You do now. Maybe there's a way we
can make some money out of this.
Then I could throw this lowlife out
of here and come home.

                    GERT
Maybe I could rent a room.

                    DEBRA
Lowlife? What are you talking
about?

MUSIC: Organ

                    ANNOUNCER (V.O.)
And what is Marian talking about?
And who could understand her anyway
from those cheap Costco false
teeth?

Marian reacts with umbrage and slowly covers
her mouth.

                    ANNOUNCER (V.O.)
And what about nosey neighbor, Nan?
What does she really have on Marian? Or does she just want to tweet
her to death?

Nan reacts in horror and tosses her cell
phone into a potted plant.

> ANNOUNCER (V.O.)
> And what about Debra, the new girl
> in town? Is she as earnest and nice
> as she claims to be? Or is she just
> a trashy slut who we'll find dead
> in the trunk of a car on some
> deserted highway?

Debra smiles but then catches herself.

> ANNOUNCER (V.O.)
> And what about me? Nobody narrates
> my life. Does anybody care about
> me?

WIDE SHOT: Everyone shakes their head, "no."

> ANNOUNCER (V.O.)
> And finally what about the stalker?
> Where is he? Is he even dead? Is he
> even a stalker or just friendly
> family doctor Leo Klein?

The front door pops open and the bandaged
Stalker just shrugs.

> ANNOUNCER (V.O.)
> For the answers to these very bit-
> ing, funny and hilarious questions
> tune in next week, "As the Stomach
> Still Turns."

END OF SCENE SIX

THE END

Kenny with Arnold . . . one more bit for the road

PHOTO CREDITS

Page 4, Kenny with Nichols & May and Marlene, 1959; collection of the author.

Page 7, Kenny with Bunk Seven, Camp Powhatan, 1952; collection of the author.

Page 8, Kenny and his Bar Mitzvah dates, 1955; photo by Clinton Saffer.

Page 14, Kenny with an unhappy Suzy Wong , 1961; collection of the author.

Page 15, Kenny with Sal Mineo at Canal Fulton Theatre, 1960; collection of the author.

Page 16, Kenny with Van Johnson in Bye Bye Birdie, Valley Forge Music Fair, 1965; collection of the author.

Page 21, Kenny and Gail, 1969; collection of the author.

Page 25, Kenny with Lily Tomlin, 1979; photo by Michael Childers.

Page 26, Kenny and Gail at the Clay Cole table, 1965; collection of the author.

Page 29, Our Wedding Album cover, 1969; illustration by Jamie Records.

Page 39, Kenny with Carol, 1967; CBS photos, collection of the author.

Page 44, Kenny with Steve Allen and Jayne Meadows, 1967; collection of the author.

Page 50, Gail and Joe and Carol and Kenny, 1967; collection of the author.

Page 54, Kenny and Vicki, 1968; CBS photos, collection of the author.

Page 57, Ethel and Carol, 1968; CBS photos, collection of the author.

Page 61, Tim and Harvey, 1968; CBS photos, collection of the author.

Page 65, Kenny and Liz, 1979; collection of the author.

Page 74, Kenny and Placido, 1983; collection of the author.

Page 75, Carol and Placido, 1983; collection of the author.

Page 75, Kenny in Carol's gown, 1983; collection of the author.

Page 82, Kenny with Betty, Adolph and Gail, 1978; collection of the author.

Page 84, *Lorelei* poster, 1974; collection of the author.

Page 86, Kenny with Danny Thomas, 1978; collection of the author.

Page 92, Lily Tomlin, 1983; NBC photos.

Page 99, Kenny with Julie Andrews, 1977; collection of the author.

Page 102, Kenny with Joan Rivers, 2009; collection of the author.

Page 104, Ellen Foley, Mimi Kennedy and Debbie Allen, 1977; NBC photos, collection of the author.

Page 107, Ad for Kelsey Grammer Special, 1996; TV Guide photos.

Page 113, The cast of *Perfectly Frank*, 1982; collection of the author.

Page 115, Kenny with Burt Bacharach, 1990; collection of the author.

Page 125, The New York company of *It Must Be Him*, 2010; collection of the author.

Page 130, Carol and Lucy in the original As The Stomach Turns, 1969; collection of the author.

Page 135, Kenny curtain call, *It Must Be Him*, 2011; photo by Jack Schaefer, collection of the author.

Page 174, Kenny with Arnold ... one more bit for the road; collection of the author.